GIANFRANCO BUSTACCHINI

RAVENNA

Mosaics, monuments and environment

Sole distributor:
CARTOLIBRERIA SALBAROLI
Via Gamba, 16 - Ravenna - Tel. 0544/32032

INTRODUCTION

Ravenna is a famous town: its monuments are known in all the world and its name is, therefore, synonym for mosaic and Byzantine art. On all the shelves of specialized and non-libraries there are a lot of volumes and magazines which are about the art and history of Ravenna, with monographs and photos; so why a new guide of Ravenna?

The books about Ravenna belong to two very distinct categories. There are the works of experts who examine Ravenna's artistic heritage in great detail as well as its historical events and archeological discoveries: thus they are products destined to be read by a distinct minority.

There are even the so-called popular guides, characterized by numerous photographs and a very brief text, often only containing the minimum, sometimes not without mistakes.

To this second group belongs the greater part of the material at present on sale, which is all very similar and leaves a sense of dissatisfaction in the visitor.

Unfortunately in Italy, unlike in anglo-saxon countries, scientific information is considered by experts as having little importance with the unfortunate result that it is often in complete and vague.

This is because, contrary to general belief, writing a simple and popular talk, requires a good knowledge of the subject enabling the speaker to explain it easily and completely.

This volume is not destined for an extremely specialized public, who will find such information elsewhere, but to those who, without identifying with the so-called «cultural visitors» wish to have, however, a more complete and exact image without being long-winded about the town of Ravenna and its surroundings such as Classe and its monuments, but also the other artistic and cultural aspects of the region.

The contents are exaustive and up-to-date and undoubtly the author will revise any future editions.

Given that there is an index, the reader will able to follow an itinerary, according to his own specific interests, without fear of missing some important monument and at the same time receiving precise but not excessive information.

A reader of this book, will have an image of Ravenna as a town imbuted with centuries of history, not only in its main points, but also in its buildings urban life and inhabitants. This is a town, which has undergone several changes, even physical and its present appearance.

Also the monuments are not unchangeable, but the remains of something of the past, still present and able to influence everyday and future reality.

MARIA GRAZIA MAIOLI

Illustration and index:
  Federico & Lino Frassinetti

Photos:
  Foto Misano di A. Ascani
  Franco Torre - Ravenna
  Daniele Camprini - Ravenna
  Ettore Malanca - Ravenna

Photographic reproduction:
  F.lli Colombo Fotolito - Milano

Glossary by:
  Patrizia Poggi

I thank Doctor M. Grazia Maioli Director of the Archaeological Service of Emilia Romagna for her assistance, Doctor Leonardo Senni, who assisted me in the preparation of the naturalistic part, my friend Daniele Camprini and the World Wildlife Found (W.W.F.) of Ravenna for its collaboration.

G. Bustacchini

An outline of the history

The origin of the town is extremely unclear. Dionysus of Alicarnasso dates it back to the Tyrrhenians, and Strabo to the Thessalians and later to the Umbrians. Nomad populations coming from he Eastern Mediterranean have been mentioned too owing to their migrations which took place between the 3rd and the Ist millennium before Christ.

It was only following the decline of Spina and Adria, trade centres, that the small primitive village began its rise as a maritime centre.

One must mention the fortunate geographic and topographic siting of Ravenna, the houses on piles are still made of wood and fishermen and salt-workers live there. Ravenna was situated on a lot of small isles, as Venice will be later, some hundred metres from the sea and sheltered from the waves by sand-dunes which occasionally left wide areas of penetration in the lagoon itself; for this reason the town was accessible to ships especially during hight tides. Moreover the big tides of the plenilune, cleaned and cleared the internal waterways and the lagoon of mud.

The Romans excluded it from their conquest of the Po valley but on seeing the high strategic value of the area, they acquired it in 89 b.C. accepting it as a federate town.

Ravenna represents an important moment in the fortunes of Rome, when in 49 B.C. Caesar gathered his troups there before crossing the Rubicon.

The outstanding position of Ravenna is not forgotten by Octavianus Augustus who decides its future after its storming during his fight with Antonius in 45 b. C. In front of a wide opening in the submerged sandbanks, on the open sea 4 km. from Ravenna he founds the military harbour of Classe, which with that of Capo Miseno on the Tyhrren is the most important harbour in the Eastern Mediterranean; the first is useful for the control of the «superum» sea, the second for the control of the «inferum» sea.

According to Dion Cassius the harbour is doubtless enormous and holds 250 ships. New hydraulic operations transformed the harbour of Classe into a river port too, thanks to a canal which connects it to the Po river and other towns which gravitate upon it such as Cremona, Piacenza and other small towns, as well as northern towns such as Aquileia.

During the Imperial Age Ravenna was positively influenced by the presence of the big harbour. At the beginning of the 2nd century, Trajan ordered the building of waterworks almost 70 km. long, (it was restored during the age of Theodoric) which at last brought water to the town from the hills near Forli.

Only a few things remain from the Golden Imperial Age at a depth of only 4-6 metre, while the foundations of the old pre-imperial walls have been found a depth of at 7 metre. But these are the 2 most important events which have left much evidence in Ravenna Today.

Ravenna, closely linked with the destiny of the Empire, reached the height of its splendour and wealth, but also of its decay in 402, when Onorio

transferred the Capital of the Western Roman Empire there from Milan. The Emperor with his court of eunuchs and corrupt cowardly nobles relied on possible help from the Eastern Empire for Ravenna; the town which with its swamps that almost entirely surround it, but an open sea in front, is without doubt a real hope for possible help from the sea.

Christianity became established in Ravenna which was brought to the eastern harbours by the harbour of Classe. It is typical that the Church of the legendary Archbishop Apollinare from Antioch, was built in the cosmopolite centre of Classe. Later Onorio transferred the bishop's seat from Classe to Ravenna.

These 2 events together will allow the development of the Church of Ravenna. Its temporal interests will be closely connected to the Imperial court and it will mantain an outstanding role over the other Italian Churches for 6 centuries, immediately following the Roman Church.

In the meantime, in 409 Alarico, king of the Visgoths invaded Italy: Ravenna was untouched, but Rome was sacked and Galla Placidia, daughter of Theodosio the Great was captured by the enemy. Alaric's successor Ataulfo married the royal hostage in Narbonne in 413 in Southern France. When Ataulfo died, Galla Placidia was given back to her brother who in 416 married her to the general Constant.

When Constant died, in order to escape from the brother who suffered from dropsy and persecuted her incestuously, she escaped to Costantinople to her uncle Theodosius, Emperor of the East; Theodosius allowed her to go back triumphant to Ravenna. Meanwhile Onozio died and Valentinian 3rd Galla Placidia's son, was the new

1 - *A panorama with the Cathedral in the middle.*

4

Western Emperor and Galla Placidia his protector.

Ravenna, with Galla Placidia had 25 years of peace. In these years «**The Basilica (*) of St. John Evangelist», the Neonian Baptistry or of the Orthodox and the so-called Mausoleum of Galla Placidia**, were built.

On 27th November 450 Augusta Galla Placidia died in Rome. In 476 the Western Roman Empire fell to Odoacre, a barbaric king who seized Ravenna. The Eastern Emperor Zenone fought against him and sent his adoptive son Theodoric, king of the Osthrogots as a hostage too; but he conquered the town and killed Odoacre after 3 years siege.

Meanwhile Ravenna was abandoned to the floods which modified the lagoon and made access to the sea difficult.

Still in 467 Sidonio Apollinare wrote a public letter to his friend which said: «Ravenna is becoming a swamp». A little bit pessimistically Procopio spoke of a dying town. The harbour of Classe had lost its importance. Venice was developing and its harbour in particular; the refugees from the Roman territories invaded by the Barbarians already lived in Venice. In spite of the bad situation Theodoric thought that Ravenna was still a safe cornerstone and settled there bringing about some benefits such as the restoration of Traianus waterways and boosting the maritime traffic. In 1938 pieces of carefully marked lead-pipeline were found and now they are exhibited at the National Museum.

The archiepiscopal chapel, the Theodoric Mausoleum (even if the Arian cult was practiced), **the church of St. Apollinare Nuovo, the Arian Baptistry,** and **the church of the Holy Spirit** date back to Theodoric age.

In Ravenna, under theodoric, who had a strong German spirit, there is a rare harmony which made it possible for Arianism and Christian Orthodox to live togetber, Latins and Gothics too, following a will aimed at a fusion of the two peoples.

But in 518, Justinian became the Eastern Emperor, he was a fanatical orthodox and in order to conquer Italy again, he began to persecute the Arians, forcing Theodoric to answer with the same cruelty.

Simmaco and Boezio (Theodoric's latin advisors) will die during this period at the court of Ravenna. In 526 Theodoric died and Ravenna was governed with numerous problems by his daughter Amalasunta, killed after a reign of 9 years.

In 535, the Eastern Emperor Justinian thought that it was the right moment for the military conquest of Italy. He sent the general Belisario to besiege Ravenna and conquer it in 540. From the seat of Ravenna the successor of Belisario started to conquer the Gothics in 554.

Justinian began to reorganize the territory and restore the damage of the bloody Gothic-Byzantine war, with the help of the archbishop Maximian; imposed on the Italian clergy by Justinian, he was a docile instrument of his.

Ravenna once again became the most important religious and politic italian town, with a high building activity. The mosaics of **St. Vitale, St. Apollinare in Classe** and a part of the church of **S. Apollinare Nuovo** (church of new S. Apollinare) dated back to the Byzantine* age. The direct relations with Byzantium went on until the 6th, 7th century and Ravenna, still under the power of the Eastern Emperor, was a vital town crowded with different people: Middle Eastern merchants, artisans, artists, dignitaries and court officials and cultured men.

5

During the long Lombard-Byzantine war, which lasted about 2 centuries, Ravenna was the operative centre of the military activities and the Emperor sent the supreme Commander of the armed forces here with the title of Exarch. This continuous war gives superiority to the exarch, in the civilian field, too, in order to be above the Imperial Prefect which was his seat in Ravenna.

In 712 Liutprand, king of the Lombards, occupied Ravenna, which after many events, returned to be Byzantine. In 741, the new king of the Lombards Astolfo, reconquered it: the Byzantine domination finished in Ravenna. The Lombards began the despoliation of the artistic wealth of Ravenna which finished only after the Napoleonic Empire, the first which reconquered the most beautiful paintings of the town.

Meanwhile Ravenna was placed 3 km. from the sea.

Pope Stephen 2nd invoked Pipino, king of the French, to free Italy from the Lombards. The Lombards were expelled, Pipino offered as his donation to the papacy, Ravenna with its Territory. Pope Adrian Ist in 784, in the name of gratitude which the Papacy owed to the Christian and liberator King Charlemagne, authorized him to take away from the buildings not subjected to the cult, and especially from Theodoric's Palace, everything he liked.

Everything trasportable was taken away savagely. From the Palace in Ravenna precious marble columns, mosaics and statues were sent to Aquisgrana (now Achen). The text of the papal authorization we know, gives the impression of a blank cheque to the french king Charlmagne who came to Ravenna 2 more times, and everytime there robbed.

In 801 he took away the equestrian statue of Theodoric. Then, Ravenna lived a fruitful period both economically and culturally (the old law school is very famous) until the IIth century, under the domination of the archbishop, among them there were the famous Pietro and Gerbert de Aurillac. They had the privilege of autocephaly from the Roman Church, obtained by the Emperor in 7th century, and sometimes they opposed the temporal authority of the Pope with violence and they succeeded in mantaining an important supremacy and independence from Rome. This is due to many benefits of the Saxon Emperors who made the Church of Ravenna the richest in Italy after the Roman one. The excommunications whic sometimes were pronounced for the archbishop of Ravenna, were ineffective.

At the end of 12th century, with the rise of the free-cities, Ravenna lost its surrounding territories and its history, as many Italian cities, was studded by fratricidal wars.

The partecipation in the fight between the Guelphes and Ghiellines increased this sad situation. Many families had power: the Traversarys, Rasponis and Polentarys, who gave hospitality to Dante during his exile, until his death and who governed from the end of 13th to the middle of 15th century.

Since 1449 for about 70 years Ravenna was under the domination of the Venetian Republic, which started the drainage, but also the deviations of the Ronco and Montone rivers, which surrounded Ravenna for defensive purposes.

This was the cause of a disastrous flood. In 1512 after the Holy League struggled Ravenna suffered a horrible sacking by the French troops.

Meanwhile the rivers surrounded the town more and more, which was frequently flooded; and the 27 and 28 May 1636 there was the great flood which reached the Basilica of St. Vitale almost 3 m. high whith hundreds of damaged and destroyed houses. For this reason, during the Papal domination, which

lasted almost 3 centuries, many hydraulic interventions were made in Ravenna. In 1739 the legate Cardinal Alberoni connected the Ronco and the Montone rivers canalizing them and he let the 2 rivers flow into the sea, 2 or 3 km. towards South from Ravenna now between Lido Adriano and Lido di Dante. The new port (Porto Corsini) was dug which has in its present course Marina di Ravenna on the right, and on the left Porto Corsini and Marina Romea.

Ravenna with its drainage works became an agricultural centre; wide surfaces of swamps and bogs became fertile land. In March 1860 the Plebiscite confirmed the annexation of Romagna to The Sardinian Reign.

The rise of the first agricultural cooperatives, anticipation of the big phenomenon of cooperation in Italy, took place in this area.

In this way when the 2nd World War finished, it was a big agricultural centre. With the opening of important chemical industries the town had to face serious problems, worsened by the progressive phenomenon of its subsidence. These problems have to be solved because this town, with such a glorious past and its monuments, must not be destroyed, its flat marshlands must not be polluted and the green pine wood must not be ruined.

---

2 - A panorama (Viale Farini, the railway-station and in the distance the end of the canal).

THE MOSAICS

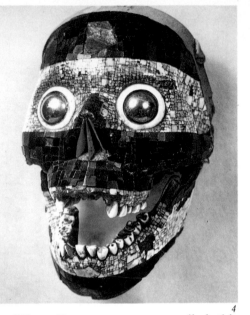

Among the oldest artistic expressions we can without doubt include the Mosaics.

Four millenniums ago the Sumerians used small dyed clay-bodies to decorate walls and columns with simple colours. The pre-Columbian civilisation of Southern and Central America and Southern Mexico, too, utilized this technique, but using different materials: semi precious stones of wonderful colors (malachite etc.) mother-of-pearl, metals and reptiles' scales. The Egyptians developed this decorative taste and they even glazed stones which were inserted in buildings and showed multicoloured figures.

The first mosaics date back to Ancient Greece, but they had few shades with animal scenes and were made of smoothed pebbles. When the Hellenistic civilisation developed, the mosaic became a very sophisticated and elaborate product, too, and a substitute for the ornamental painting.

Complicated figure scenes, dead nature, mithologic episodes are also made with uncommon materials such as onyx, serpentine, glass paste etc.

When Roman power prevailed this form of art was absorbed by the winners which spread it abroad in every part of the Empire from Northern Africa to the Blak sea, from Asia to Spain. Mosaics made by famous Greek Mosaicists were in the houses of rich patricians in Rome and other cities.

The material most used by the Romans was made by **«Tesserae»** (the small cubes of which a mosaic is composed) of calcareus rocks, but glass material was also used, where the colour intensity of the nature rock was not bright enough.

Moreover, there is another important aspect: the Roman mosaicists exceeded the limit imposed on the Mosaic by the Hellenistic tradition of the expressive phenomenon, and it was shown as a decorative element in order to establish architectural space with colour.

The Mosaic brought by the Romans had a general and standard characteristic even if it changed according to the school of origin.

Above all the use of the **Floor mosaic** was so frequent, that in the 3rd century the Emperor Diocletian fixed the prices for the mosaicists according to the various levels of qualification including the «*Lapidarius stuctor*» and the «*calcis*

8

5

coctor» that is to say the manual labourers.

Then, when in 330 A. D. the Emperor Costantin transferred the Imperial Seat from Rome to Byzantium, particular facilities were given to the Greek and Roman mosaicists, such as tax exemption thus encouraging the exodus to the new capital. This event contributed to the important turning point in mosaic development, which blended with the Eastern artistic tradition, and developed an evolution of mosaic tradition from the 5th century onwards, of which the most spectacular and spontaneous characteristic is the generalized use of the big golden painting in the background.

Ravenna, a meeting point for the Western and the Eastern World, hands us down these extraordinary testimonies, which survived the iconoclast age (in 726 the veneration of images was forbidden) with the **classic mosaics of Christian art** (Galla Placidia 5th century) and **Truly Byzantine** (the procession of the Virgin and martyrs. New St. Apollinare 6th century).

Unfortunately a great part of that marvellous golden age of the mosaic has disappeared. The mosaics of the Holy Cross, of the Basilica Apostolorum (nowadays St. Francis) of the Anastasis Gothorum (nowadays: the Holy Spirit), of St. John the Evangelist of St. Agatha the Elder, of St. Michael in Africisco have disappeared; the Basilica Ursiana, St. Lawrence in Cesarea, the Basilica Petriana have disappeared with the buildings which housed them. In 1200 during the 4th crusade with the taking of Constantinople, Venice aided the recovery of Byzantine and Greek artists and artisans those from Ravenna who by moving to Venice started the glass tradition which still exists today. In 8th century the use of mosaic as an artistic, autonomous expression began to diminish, in 9th century it was abandoned and replaced by the Fresco, by the painting on canvas and Panels. At the end of the last century in Ravenna a tradition of restoration was almost spontaneously born in order to preserve its mosaics; this tradition, began with Novelli and Zampiga, has continued for 25 years with the Mosaicists Group (now a cooperative) which is already well known in the national and international field.

In Ravenna there is the headquarters of the International Association of the Contemporary Mosaicists, in order to demonstrate that Modern Art, which is always in search of new expressive means, has discovered this old form of art right in Ravenna.

---

3 - *The two-faced banner of Ur (Mesopotamia) a scene of war and peace. It is the most ancient mosaicwork up-to-now. III millenium B.C. (British Museum). In tesseras of mother-of-pearl, lapislazuli, schist and pink stone.*

4 - *Death's head (the divinity Tezcatlipoca) in tesseras of turquoise and obsidian.*

5 - *Dyonisius on a panther (Delos- House of the Masks- end of the II century B.C.).*

9

PIAZZA DEL POPOLO

On the western side of the square 2 columns were erected in 1483 during the short Venetian Domination. The rise of the steps was sculptéd in bas-relief* by Pietro Lombardo with the signs of the zodiac and allegorical figures.

On the northern column* there is the baroque statue of **St. Vitale** as a soldier, with the helm and the pike made by Clemente Melly and on the southern one there is **St. Apollinaris,** both patrons of Ravenna.

Since 1644 St. Vitale replaced the lion of St. Mark which was put on top of the column by the Venetian republic (la Serenissima).

The town hall

It was rebuilt in 1681, then restored and in part modified in 1765 and in 1857; with this last intervention the architect Albino Riccardi invented the merlons which have also given the name to the town hall of crenellated hall.

The town hall is connected by a big vault* to the **Venetian hall** built by the Venetians in 1461. It rests on 6 big granite columns with capitals* of the 6th century coming from the Church of St. Andrew of the Goths which was demolished by the Venetians in order to widen the big fortification, the socalled «Rocca Brancaleone» still existent. **The monogram of Theodoric** in legible on 3 capitals; the best preserve is the first on the right side coming from Via Cairoli.

The big fresco painted by Adolfo De Carolis in 1921 on the high facade has disappeared due to dampness and brackish air.

At the end of the square there is the building with the **Clock tower.** In 1785

the architect from Ravenna Camillo Morigia restored the building which dated back to 1483. The style is neoclassic. Near there is the Suffragio church erected at the beginning of 18th century, but it was modified many times by the same architect Camillo Morigia. The square is a meeting point for the town and is particularly crowded on Saturday morning, market day. Ravenna in spite of its industries has remained a great agricultural town and on Saturday morning the square is thronged with farmers, breeders, dealers and brokers who have their contracting place here.

The bell-tower* dated back to 15th century, of **St. Michael in Africisco**

6 - *Piazza del Popolo.*
7 - *Piazza del Popolo with the Town Hall and the Venetian Palace.*
8 - *Venetian Palace: capital of the destroyed Church of St. Andrew of the Goths with monogram of Theodoric.*

11

9

church can be seen walking along Via 4 Novembre, on the left hand on reaching number 39.

The bell-tower and the polygonal apse* (in the private yard of number 33) are the remains of the old church built during Justinian's Empire, while the Basilica of St. Vitale (547) and St. Apollinare in Classe were being built.

This church was dedicated to St. Michael the Archangel and consecrated by Maximian; it was ordered by a rich banker Julian a silversmith and a relative of his Bacauda. We will talk about Julian visiting the Basilica of St. Vitale more at length. The church was deconsecrated in 1805 and bought by a private citizen for 80 scudi in order to make small shops there.

Then, he sold the beautiful mosaic for 300 scudi of the apse to the envoy of the king of Prussia Fredrick William 4th after having obtained permission from Pope Gregory 16th.

It was brought to Venice, then to Berlin and after 60 years it was displayed at the Early Christian Art Museum. Any visitor who wishes to see it, even if unnatural and widely restored, can find it at the «Staatliche Museum». We have underlined these details in order to say that the artistic wealth of Ravenna and the Italian one have been the purpose of many spoliations, which sometimes were brutal, sometimes hidden, or as happens in this century, with real trade transactions allowing important old works of art to become the wealth of important foreign museums.

9 - *Decorations in the vault between Piazza del Popolo and Piazza XX Settembre made by Gaetano Savini of Ravenna in 1873 with famous persons of Ravenna.*

10 - *Bell-tower of the church of S. Michele in Africisco.*

12

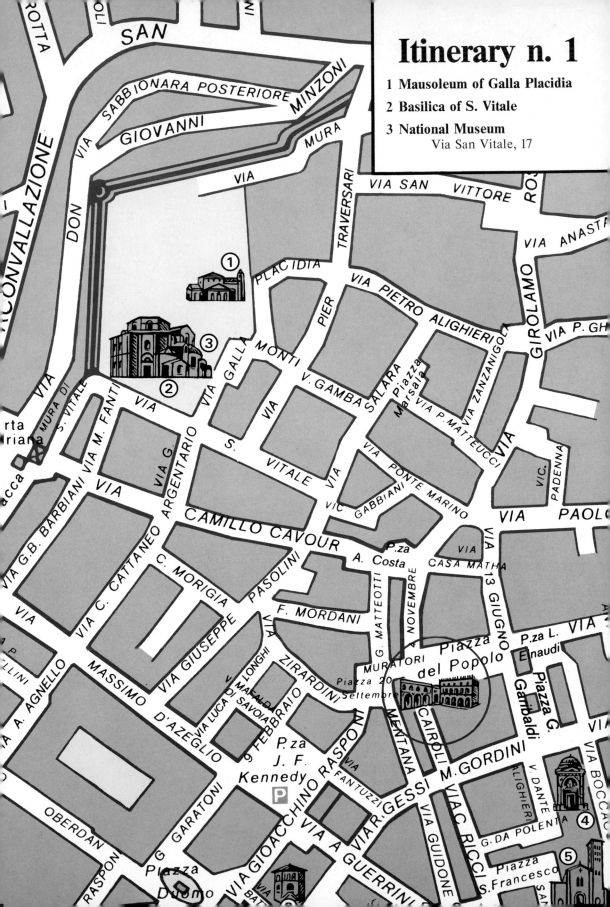

Itinerary n. 1

1 **Mausoleum of Galla Placidia**

2 **Basilica of S. Vitale**

3 **National Museum**
   Via San Vitale, 17

GALLA PLACIDIA MAUSOLEUM

(5th century)

At the beginning of the 5th century, the move of the imperial seat from Milan to Ravenna, made the development of many sacred buildings possible, and naturally the Imperial Palace and the Palatine Chapel (Holy Cross).

The development of this mausoleum enlarged the surface of the Roman city. Perhaps these buildings are on the side of the town where the Imperial quarters were placed.

In the introduction we spoke about Galla Placidia as a Historical figure: thus, this outline helps the introduction to the description of the monument built between 425 and 430, after the return of Galla Placidia from Bisanzio to Ravenna. The visitors will be astonished

at the contrast between the simple outside in brickwork of Roman origins, enriched with pilasters*, small arches and tympana*, and the inside decorated with wonderful mosaics of Classic Roman-Hellenistic taste, they are the oldest and most complete of the mosaics of Ravenna.

We are not sure that Augusta Galla Placidia was buried in this small building in the shape of a latin cross. The exact purpose of this building was for an oratory dedicated to St. Lawrence; he was particularly venerated in Ravenna so that 3 churches in Ravenna were dedicated to him. (St. Lawrence in Cesarea, St. Lawrence in Posterula and St. Lawrence in Pannonia).

This sacellum is isolated now, but it was a part of the Holy Cross church of a previous age, which can be seen on the other side of the narrow street behind the mausoleum.

In 1602, in order to create the present Galla Placidia Street, a part of the church was destroyed and the Holy Cross façade was shortened, isolating the small sacellum of Galla Placidia in this way. **The barrel shaped** vault at the entrance is beautiful and deep blue, with circular golden decorations representing white corollas of moonflowers which lighten the deep quiet of the blue sky. The mosaicists who worked here, have not forgotten that the Romans used precious and coloured materials in order to adorn the walls of civil and in particular religious buildings.

The mosaicists of Ravenna and in particular the Galla Placidia ones do not carry out, as the Greek and the Roman wall mosaic a pictorial function, but they are an integral and complete part of the architectonic structure subordinately. At the end of the vault there is

the **central intrados*** adorned with a **festoon* of flowers and fruits,** bursting from a basket intertwined with gold full of rushes and fresh fruit; apples, grapes, and pomegranates. Behind, above the entrance door there is **The Good Shepherd** with a calm face, young and without a beard with golden tunic, his purple mantle, the big cross and the big golden halo* is situated on the rocks among 6 small sheep.

The landscape is very peaceful, rich with plants and flowers. Its place near the entrance has an allusive meaning: only through Christ can we reach eternal peace.

The dome

There is a golden cross with the base turned towards the East, in a golden starry sky. On the 4 sides, on the **sprandels,** there are **the golden symbols of the 4 Evangelists,** repositories of the New Revelation, rising from coloured cirri: St. Mark's Lion, St. Luke's Ox, St. John's eagle, and the man of St. Matthew. The use of symbolic figures such as the lion, the ox, the eagle and man, has very old roots which Christianity has taken from Eastern pagan mythology. St. Mark begins to narrate speaking about the lion, St. Luke exalts the sacrifice of which the ox is the first representative, St. John considers the eagle as the ruler of the sky and contemplation, St. Matthew in particular talks about Christ as a man. Then, the artist-mosaicist represented the sky deeper, declining into a perspective play, so that the gigantic stars around the 4 symbols of the Evangelist descend around the cross.

Below, in the **lunettes* of the drum** there are Apostles in couples on a blue background, with white tunics, who venerate the cross above them. In **the lunette on the left** we see St. Paul and St. Peter with a key in his hand.

At his feet each one has a vase or a

11 - Mausoleum of Galla Placidia.

12

small fountain where white doves are quenching their thirst. The spirits in search of eternal peace try to find refreshment and quench their thirst at the salvation fountain.

The doves, the fish (the oldest Christian symbol), the palms and others repeated motives represent common symbols in Christian symbology. The dove is the announcer of Heavenly Peace (with the olive branch), it is the image of the Christian spirit because of its candour and sweetness; it is the image of the spirit which has conquered the kingdom of heaven when in his mouth there is the laurel.

On the edge, there are wine-shoots in order to remind the close union between Christian people and Christ (I am the wine and you are the shoots).

In **the frontal lunettes,** there is St. Lawrence with the cross of martyrdom on his shoulders and he is going to be put on the grill, as the Christian hagiography says.

In the *underside of the arch** there is a Greek* key in beautiful colours, of particular interesting actuality.

In **the lunettes of the lateral wings** there are 2 deer with big horns which are watering themselves, almost wrapped by achantus* volutes. They are the chatecumens* which find refreshment in the water of Baptism. Once again the

---

12 - *The barrel-shaped vault and the Good Shepherd.*
13 - *The Good Shepherd seated among the lambs (detail).*

16

13 ▶

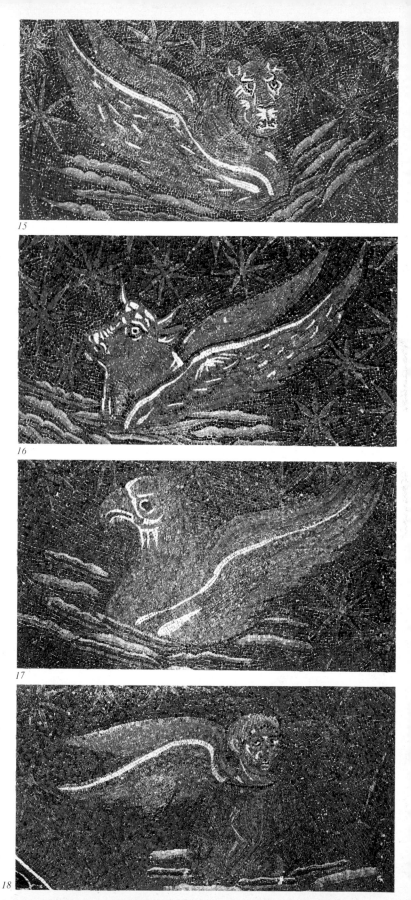

15

16

17

14 - The golden Cross in the starry
     sky of the dome.
15 - 16 - 17 - 18 - The symbols of the
     Evangelists: The St. Mark's
     lion, the St. Luke's ox, the St.
     John's eagle and the St. Mat-
     tew's Man.

19

◀ 14

18

19

Christian symbology represents salvation with water from a spring whose surface is ruffled by the light waves.

All around there are a lot of flowers. After the visit to the mosaics we go to see the marble **sarcophaguses** placed in the 3 small niches.

There is a great deal of literature about these sarcophaguses, but it is almost certain that their dimension, the iconographic figures intercurrent between the mosaic decoration and the decoration of the principal part of the sarcophaguses were built and adapted in order to be preserved within them.

The sarcophagus of Galla Placidia is considered the one in front of the entrance. It is surely the most important, even if it seems vulgar and incomplete because it is a reutilized Roman sepulchre. Several deep holes on the front could be used to keep cramps destined to keep precious marble and metals. On the front and on the back there are 2 impressions of ansate

19 - *The drinking doves (detail).*
20 - *The sarcophagus called of Galla Placidia.*

20

«tabulae» which were never sculpted. It is said that in the 16th century someone made a big hole to look inside the sarcophagus, that can be seen in the back part below, and used a straw or a lighted candle; this could have caused the destruction of the mummified remains and the covering in resinous wood. The sarcophagus on the left is considered maybe wrongly, the sepulchre of the general Constant 3rd, husband of Augusta Galla Placidia; on the front there are 2 sculpted lambs with the monogram of Constantine, with the apostles Peter and Paul. From the Hill of Heaven flow down the 4 rivers. The haloed Mystic Lamb is on the hill with the monogram of Constantine, too.

The sarcophagus on the right with the lid as a trunk could have belonged to Valentinian 3rd, or to Honorius Galla Placidia's brother. The front is divided into 3 small chapels of pagan origin, and represents the Mystic Lamb(as in Galla Placidia's) on the Hill of Heaven, with 2 doves on the cross.

21 - *General view.*
22 - *The fountain (detail).*
23 - *The Apostle St. Peter (detail of the left lunette).*

23

25

26

24 - *The surpraising modernity of the Greek fret under the arch.*
25 - *Sarcophagus of Constant III, on the left at the entrance.*
26 - *Sarcophagus of Valentinian III on the right of the entrance.*

25

 24

THE BASILICA OF ST. VITALE

(6th century)

It was begun under Gothic domination by the bishop Ecclesio in 527, then it was finished by the 27th bishop of Ravenna Maximian, who consecrated it on 17 May 548 under Byzantine domination. The Basilica of St. Vitale represents an extraordinary example of Byzantine architecture filtered from the architectural experiences of Rome and Ravenna, in which the baldness of the buildings and the decorative function of the mosaics led to a very good result, the one and only in the World.

Building elements of Roman tradition (the tecnique of the dome, the entrance door shaped like a forceps, and the stepped towers) can be found there, but there are also the capitals, the transennas* and the polygonal apse clearly of Byzantine Origin. We also find here, as in the Basilica of St. Apollinare in Classe a generous banker of Greek origin, Julian the silversmith, he is supposed to be the banker who paid 26000 golden solidus for the building of the basilica.

Many things have been said about this mysterious man, and because of the large amount of money for the Church's building (St. Vitale and St. Apollinare in Classe). It is possible that the Eastern Emperor helped these works in order to pave the way for the conquest of Ravenna and Italy. It was very common during ancient times for rich people to finance religious buildings; these operation were regulated by the Imperial decree which established all the details of the different stages (the duration of the work, the exact amount of money and the obligations of the heirs in order to assure the total execution of the works tc.).

The Basilica has a central plant not common among the Christian Western Churches; the building is surmounted by a dome which outside is octagonal, while on the side of the apse many round sloping and squared buildings were projected in which the deacon* and the prothesis* were placed.

The window which now has normal painted glass, originally had coloured discoidal glass, of which some samples have been found during excavations and now they are in the National Museum.

The thin bricks 4 cm. high, arc typical of the Justinian age, fixed with a layer of lime of the same thickness. The **bell tower,** a raising of one of the 2 stepped towers, dates back to 10th century; it was half destroyed by the earthquake in 1688 and was rebuilt after a few years, but it was also restored in the middle of 18th century. The **big counterforts** which contain the bases of the vaults dated back to 1000.

The entrance to the Basilica is not the original which took through the arcaded court now covered by the second cloister of the National Museum dates back to 6th century; since the beginning of the century the narthex* can be seen; thus, it is deprived of its original marbles and curiously oblique in comparison with the axis of the Basilica; this obliquity was explained by the necessity to

---

27 - *Basilica of S. Vitale.*

28 - *On page 28-29: general view of the right of the Presbitery.*

26

incorporate previous votive chapels. The dome of 16 m. diameter was built, like many other monuments of this period, with clay tubes inserted one inside the other, horizontally placed; the clearly Mediterranean and Byzantine tecnique allows an easy and rapid building. Inside, the 8 big pillars* create 8 big niches on which the dome is placed, it was frescoed in the 16th century, but totally repainted by the Bolognese Ubaldo Gandolfi for the figures and Serafino Gandolfi for the ornamental part. The frescoes were finished by the Venetian Giacomo Guarana, in great contrast with the mosaics. The 8 big niches are occupied above by the upper ambulatory or women's gallery (the entrance is from the stepped tower), place of prayer reserved for women and by the lower ambulatory, both end at the presbytery*. The architectonic rhythm strikes the visitor for its wideranging of apses and the slenderness of the vault, but also for the splendor of the mosaic frame and the strange veins of the pillar's marble in a perfect harmony.

The capitals of the lgwer portics shaped like a basket and sculpted like lotus leaves, have on the pulvins monograms with different interpretations.

29

29 - *Byzantine capital and stuccos of the*
underarch.

30 - *Presbytery: the bust of Christ in the middle of*
the intrados.

30

The mosaics of the Presbytery

In the intrados, the medallions with busts of Christ, as an ideal concept of the offertory; are in the middle of the arch of the 12 apostles of St. Gervase and St. Protasio; the legend says that they are sons of the centurion St. Vitale and St. Valery. They dress a tunic and a pallium*. The green intertwined dolphins under each medallion are in a composition of rare equilibrium and taste and examples of the fertile imagination of the school of Ravenna, of the «Pictor imaginarius» that is to say of the author of themes to tell with mosaics; all is framed with decorations of good chromatic quality. The dolphin, tranquil dweller of waves means salvation in this representation.

In the **domical vault** the central medallion is striking; it is shaped like a wreath of leaves, apples, pears, and the haloed mystic lamb on a background of golden stars.

This medallion is supported by 4 angels literally sunk in green vaults of acanthus leaves whose tree comes out from the middle of every gore, animated with a multitude of animals, from the duck to the donkey from the cock to the swallow.

At the corner, 4 peacocks show their beautiful tails opened like a fan.

The peacock in Christian symbology represents the Resurrection because it renews the splendor of its mantle each spring and moreover it is the symbol of immortality because it was thought that its flesh was imputrescible. After the earthquake Of July 1781 a part of the vault fell down and the painter of the dome was charged to copy the mosaic. In 1922 the operation was redone by the teacher restorer Zampiga and in 1963 restored by the mosaicists group of Ravenna.

The final result of the restoration with the finishing in tempera, allows a complete and exhaustive sight of the original and whole decoration. The 2 **lateral walls** are characterized by an extraor-

31

32

33

31 - Presbytery: St. Gervase.
32 - Presbytery: St. Protasio.
33 - Ibis (detail of the vault of the Presbytery).
34 - The domical vault of the Presbytery with the haloed Mystic Lamb in the starry background.

32

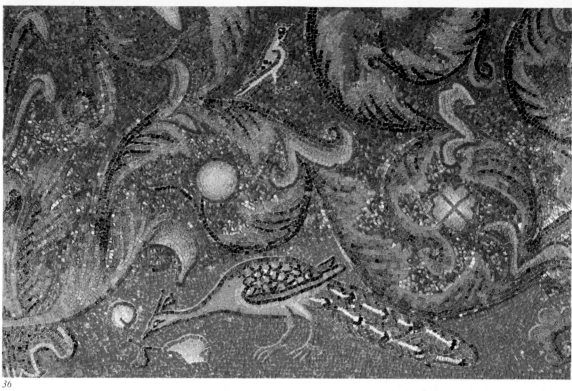

36

37

35 - Upper part on the left of the
Presbitery: Cantharus, vine and
doves.
36 - Domical vault of the Presbytery:
peacock.
37 - Domical vault of the Presbytery:
coupled doves.

35

dinary lightness due to the 2 three light windows* enriched by fretworked capitals, which enlighten the 2 big mosaic paintings in the background.

In the **left lunette** there are 2 episodes of Abraham's life: the Angels seated at the table* under a leafy oak, announce the birth of his son Isaac to Abraham, while Sarah at the hut door is smiling with her finger on her mouth owing to her great surprise, in the nearby scene the Patriarch Abraham is going to sacrifice his own son with a shield in his hand, while the hand of God stops the armed arm. The richness of the details and the completeness of the images should be noted, which never leave an empty space; everywhere there are big trees, grass and flowers, anticipators of the wide flowered field of the Basilica of St. Apollinare in Classe.

In the supports there is the prophet Jeremiah on one side, and on the other side there is Moses who receives the sacred Tablets on Mount Sinai. At the bottom, there is Aaron, Moses' brother,

with the heads of the 12 tribes of Israel in rebellion. The decoration around the upper three light windows formed by 2 beautiful onyx columns with pulvinate* capitals, represents the Evangelists on the right Luke with the Apocalyptic Symbol of the ox above his head and on the left John with the eagle. The landscape is rocky. Unlike the same figures of Galla Placidia's Mausoleum, here the ox and the eagle are entirely

---

38 - Left lunette of the Presbytery: episodes of the Abraham's life.
39 - Presbytery: detail of the life of Abraham in which the Angels announce to Abraham the birth of the son Isaac.

40

42

40 - Presbytery: detail of the life of Abraham (Abraham and Sarah).
41 - Presbytery: detail of the life of Abraham (Abraham helps to sacrifice his son Isaac).
42 - Presbytery: the Prophet Jeremiah.
43 - Presbytery: (left side) Moses receives the sacred tables on the Mount Sinai.

38

43 ▶

44 - Presbytery (Left side): St. Luke the Evangelist.

45 - Presbytery (left side): St. John the Evangelist.

46 - Presbytery (left side): Aron with the chiefs of the 12 tribes of Israel.

47 - Detail of the window with three openings on the left side of the Presbytery.

40

represented exceeding in this way the zoomorfic attribute in order to mantain the natural'sm of the scene below on which there is Luke near 2 puddles in which 2 herons are moving and John with 2 ducks.

Above these pictures in the **extrados*** of the lunette there are doves with 2 vases from which 2 wine-shoots rise which decrease more and more reaching the cross in the middle of the arch.

On the **right lunette,** there is the sacrifice of Abel who going out from a hut covered in an animal skin and a red mantle, he offers a lamb as in the sacrifice; on the other side of the altar enriched by a wide white sheet there is Melchizedek dressed as a priest who offers bread and wine while he is going out from a temple.

In the support, there is Moses who leads the flock to Jetro the priest; Moses is entering the burning bush taking off his sandals; on the right there is the prophet Isaiah.

Around the upper three light window there is St. Matthew on the left and St. Mark on the right with pen and ink-pot with his 2 symbols; the winged man and the lion. There is a naturalistic touch here, too, rocks, puddles and a turtle which swims around the feet of the heron.

The onyx columns of the upper three light window have the pulvin with a relief medallion with the deciphered monogram of Julian the silversmith, the backer of the Basilica.

The upper part of the apsidal extrados with the beautful three light windows is luxuriant with wine-shoots which rise from 2 vases and fall into 2 baskets; below there are 2 flying angels who have a multicoloured circle with 7 rays coming from the central alpha.

On the right side and on the left one there are the begemmed walls of Bethlehm and Jerusalem preceded by 2 green cypresses. We again find, the symbology of St. Apollinare in Classe in the identification with 2 cities which represent the history of the Salvation of Man.

41

48

49

50

48 - *Right lunette of the Presbytery: the sacrifices of Abel and Melchizedeck.*
49 - *Detail of the offering of the bread and the wine of Melchizedeck.*
50 - *Detail of the sacrifice of Abel.*

42

50 ▶

51

52

53

54

---

51 - *Right side of the Presbytery: Moses leads the herd of the priest Jetro.*
52 - *Right side of the Presbytery: St. Mattew.*
53 - *Right side of the Presbytery: St. Mark.*
54 - *Right side of the Presbytery: The Prophet Isaiah.*
55 - *Right side of the Presbytery: Moses is going to enter the oakwood on fire.*

44

56

57

46

58

56 - *Right side of the Presbytery: The lion, symbol of St. Mark the Evangelist.*
57 - *Right side of the Presbytery: detail of the decoration.*
58 - *Right side of the Presbytery: detail of the heron and the tortoise.*

59

60

59 - *Apsidal estrados: both angels hold up the circle with Alpha in the middle.*

60 - *Apsidal estrados: the bejewelled walls of Bethlehem.*

61 - *Apsidal estrados: the walls of Jerusalem.*

49

The apse mosaics

The mosaic decoration of the conch unlike that in the presbytery of clear Hellenistic-Roman influence, shows traces in the distempered golden background of Byzantine influence. The underside of the arch is decorated with cornucopias paired with flowers and birds.

In the middle of **the apsidal bowl-shaped vault** there in the young and beardless Reedimer, who has in his hand the roll with the 7 seals, sitting on the celestial globe (the creation) at his sides there are 2 angels and he offers the martyr's crown to St. Vitale (on his right), he wears a wonderful regal mantle (St. Vitale was martyrized under Diocletian and his relics were exhumed in St. Ambrose's presence).

On the left there is the bishop Ecclesio, promoter of the Basilica who is offering the Church to Christ; he has the model of the church in his hand.

The field which represents the celestial garden is rich with flowers with the 4 stylized rivers in the shape of an interwining and the sky covered with multicoloured cirri; this garden has the same mosaic decoration of that in the Basilica of St. Apollinare in Classe. The complex composition is perfectly inserted in the wide surface of the apse.

At the bottom there are the famous mosaic panels of the Emperor Justinian on the left, and of the Empress Theodora on the right.

63

64

62 - *The under arch of the apse: Decoration with cornucopias, birds and flowers.*
63 - *Bowl-shaped vault of the apse with in the middle the Redeemer seating on the celestial globe.*
64 - *Detail of the apsidal bowl-shaped vault: St. Vitale in the act of receiving the crown of the glory of the martyrdom.*

51

Justinian

The Emperor with a golden paten* in his hand, the purple mantle, and the halo, symbol of the Imperial power of divine origins, goes to the place of sacrifice preceded by the archbishop Maximian, representative of imperial religious politics, he has in his hand a big cross and wears a pallium like a stole; a deacon holds the Gospel and the subdeacon holds the incense. The scene was surely ordered by Maximian, it has the characteristic of a symbolic cerimony and of dedication in order to confirm the piety and the devotion to the cult of the Emperor Justinian and of the Empress Theodora who never went to Ravenna; in this scene the imperial authority of Byzantium and the Church of Ravenna are united only in a homage.

Because of the great diligence with the figures have been made it is difficult to think that the subjects are only a fruit of imagination; in fact Maximian identificable for the inscription of clear dalmatic origin, was painted with his distinguishing marks (tall, half bald, blue eyes and hollow face). The mosaicist who painted him, had without doubt the chance to look at this important figure carefully.

65 - *Left side of the apse: large representation with the Emperor Justinian.*

65

Maximian, deacon of Pola and successor to the archbishop Victor of Ravenna, was consecrated in 546 by Pope Virgil and elected responsible for the dioceses of Milan and Aquileia by the Emperor Justinian. The man between Maximian and Justinian could be Julian the Silversmith, just as the dignitary on the left of the Emperor could be the general Belisario, winner against the Gothics.

66 - *Detail of the Archbishop Maximian.*
67 - *Detail of the Emperor Justinian.*

54

Theodora

The Empress opens the procession; the historians say that she was previously a dancer and a prostitute. She has her head surrounded by the halo, symbol of power of divine origin. A goblet covered with gems and pearls is in her hand, while a courtier raises the curtain and shows the gushing water of the fountain.

Her sumptuous purple dress abounds with golden embroideries, among which those of the lower border which represent the Three Kings with the gifts: this decoration reconfirms, in this small detail, too, Justinian and Theodora's fidelity to the King of Heaven, towards which they put the gifts, as the Three Kings did. A diadem covered with nacre completes the image of the pomp of Byzantium court. Behind Theodora's head there is a shelled niche, Christian* symbol of immortality. Near Theodora there are other figures which the tradition tells as Antonina, general Belisario's wife and their daughter Giovannina.

The great image of Theodora, the same as that of the Emperor should not astonish; us in fact it is known that she had a great importance and ascendancy on her husband and perhaps on Maximian who was very grateful to her.

In the same apse in the lower part under the 3 windows there are compartments with **marble inlayings** glassy enamels, gold and nacre spaced with pilasters in green serpentine.

68 - Right side of the apse: large representation of the Empress Theodora.

68

The first and the last slab are original; the others are beautiful rebuildings dating back to the beginning of 1900 by means of hard stones mill of Florence. On both sides of the panel there is the monogram of Julian the silversmith, the financer banker of the Basilica.

The altar has an alabaster mensa with a beautiful transparency, reassambled in 1898, coming from the nearby church of Holy Cross, it was ordered by Galla Placidia in 425.

The 2 **marble compositions** at the base of the intrados on a side of the altar date back to the 16th century; they are composed by 2 **Roman pagan bas-reliefs** representing Neptune's throne and by beautiful columns; one of those is made of precious green Egyptian breccia; it sustained the old canopy* or baldachin of the altar.

Between the 2nd and the 3rd pilaster on the left of the entrance there is a cavity in the floor (*the socalled well*) always full of water coming from a bed of a river. It is considered the original burial place of St. Vitale's relics.

69 - *Detail of the fountain.*
70 - *Detail of the Empress Theodora.*

58

70 ▶

In fact in 1912 traces of the sacellum with a mosaic floor, the base of the altar, the altar with a small well with the relics of St. Vitale, dated back to the 5th century were found here. The original mosaic is near this place, and was reassambled on a metallic framing by means of the mosaicists group. Thus, it is proved that the present Basilica incorporated the old sacellum of the martyr St. Vitale.

On the left of the entrance there is a beautiful **sarcophagus** with a lid shaped like a trunk dating back to the 5th century belonging to the *Armenian exarch Isacio,* on the front there is a representation in high relief*, unusual for the funerary art of Ravenna; the Three Kings with the Phrygian cap and the fluttering mantle, bring gifts to the Virgin Mary and Christ while a star shines in the sky. At both sides Daniel among the lions and the miracle of St.

Lazarus's Resurrection; behind there are 2 peacocks and Christ's monogram. Along the short exit path there are some examples of sarcophaguses, some are utilized but not inscribed without the dead man's inscription. Near the gate there is a Roman example dating back to the 3rd century, finished in its standard working and ready to sell. In the front there are some faces to sculpt. The usage of these sepulchres was so frequent that the stonecutters kept ready also sarcophaguses with images to establish at the moment of death.

---

71 - *Sarcophagus named of the Armenian Exarch Isacio (V century).*
72 - *Greek crater with figures recovered in the necropolis of St. Martino in Gattara (Brisighella).*

NATIONAL MUSEUM

The entrance is in the garden between the Basilica of St. Vitale and the Mausoleum of Galla Placidia.

The material kept here, comes from the central nucleus gathered by the friar Pietro Canneti from Camaldoli at the beginning of the 18th century in the Classense Library. The collection became the property of the town (Ravenna) then it was reorganized by the sculptor from Ravenna Enrico Pozzi, then it became State property. The display is the following: at **the first floor** there are collections of old weapons, archaeological finds of areas near Ravenna; **in the 2 cloisters,** there are fragments and architectonical parts of different ages, in particular Roman funerary finds. **At the upper floor** there are: Roman sculptures, prehistoric material, small bronzes, glasses, coins and medals, old materials, ivories, ceramics and icons.

Ground floor

In the entrance hall a lot of armours and different weapons of 16th and 17th century are displayed.

In the 2nd hall there are the finds of the necropolis of St. Martino in Gattara, (Brisighella). In this small town, near the border with Tuscany, on the banks of the river Lamone, during the excavation from 1951 to 1963 many tombs were found dating back probably to the Umbrians of 6th and 5th century b. C. They are iron and bronze weapons and clay materials and crockery. Some pots are of clear Greek origin, in particular the beatiful crater with figures.

In the second part of the same hall there are urns and incinerations made of fired bricks and glass found during the excavation of 1966, near St. Severo Basilica of Classe in Via Romea Vecchia. There are necropolis of sailors (Classiarii) of the Roman Imperial fleet dating back to Ist century A.D.

The ambler steles with the sculpted title of these classarii are very interesting: an axe to indicate the chief carpenters or the rudder for the helmsman. We reach the **cloister** of Reinassance style with a beautiful coupled columns*, built by Andrea della Valle in 1562.

There are a lot of fragments of Roman, early Christian, Byzantine, Gothic, Reinassance and baroque buildings. At the end of the way of this cloister on round bases of fired bricks there are beautiful Corinthian-Byzantine capitals; some round and swallen acanthus leaves come from the the church of St. Andrew of the Gothic of which we see other examples on the columns of the Venetian Palace in

72

61

73

74

Piazza del Popolo. One of these, too, has the monogram of King Theodoric quite visible.

There is also a big sarcophagus of the 5th century. A scene quite common for the sarcophaguses of Ravenna is sculpted on the front that is the "*Traditio Legis*" or the consignment of the Law by means of Christ; on the outside of the 2 big trunks of the palms, there are 2 figures which seem extraneus to the common iconography; they should be the image of the orderers of the sarcophagus. On the right side there is Daniel between 2 lions and on the left the miracle of Lazarus Resurrection. Under the sarcophagus and fixed on the wall there is a slab used as a draining-board for corpses near there is a shorter slab with the cavities to lean the head. Both are dated back to the 5th century. The 2nd Reinassance cloister was partly restored after the damage of the 2nd World War which also damaged some finds. There are funerary steles, part of

73 - *Pediment of a large sarcophagus of the V century with the «Traditio Legis».*
74 - *Side of the same sarcophagus with the Resurrection of Lazarus.*
75 - *Corinthian-Byzantine capital of the vanished church of St. Andrew of the Goths with the monogram of Theodoric.*

62

75

sarcophaguses and funeral pillars found in the necropolis near the Basilica of St. Apollinare in Classe, dating back to the Ist, 2nd and 3rd century B. C. Many of these steles remind us that Classe, merchant and naval port, had a cosmopolitan popoulation, but clearly determined in the organized Roman System.

There are a lot of epigraphs of «Classarii» coming from Dalmatia and Pannonia (not yet invaded by the Magyars, the present Hungary) Syria and Egypt.

Just on the right side there is a stele with niches belonging to the family Firmia and Latronia (Ist century A. D.) on which the members of the family are represented, there is also a young man called Sperato with the indication "verna" which means slave born by his oweners.

On the same side there is the well known tripartite stele of Publio Longidieno (Ist century) who let himself represented in a boat-yard while is working with an axe to a small boat. Thus, the stele's holder is a "faber navalis" that is to say a ship's carpenter. In 1588 it was found as a common marble slab walled inside the town walls.

The previous stele is the funeral pillar of Falleo the helmsman (gubernator) of the ship called Galatea. The 2 most valuable pieces are in the same side: they are 2 sculptural fragments of Parian marble found under the floor of the mausoleum of Galla Pacidia and it should be a part of an altar of Claudius Age.

It is know as "apoteosi di Augusto" (Augustus' deification) because of the right figure, the highest, which could be the Emperor Augustus with the characteristics of Jupiter. The research of physical and plastic perfection made by the sculptor has surely modified the characteristics of Claudius-Julius family and in this way the identification of the single characters is problematical. The star on the forehead of the nude boy should be death.

The smallest fragment, a part of the other nearby, reproduces a scene in which a richly harnessed ox taken by the slaves "vittimari" is brought to the sacrifice.

In the *first small* room there are 2 big pateras* coming from the disappeared Porta Aurea (Golden Gate) built by the Emperor Claudius in 43 A.D. and demolished by the Venetians to obtain building material; around they are finely sculpted with a wreath of oak leaves and inside with an ornamental motif with palms; they give the idea of the majesty of this gate from which the "Via Decumana" started.

In the following small room, there are some finds of the Roman villa of Russi, 17 km. from Ravenna (on the way to Faenza), with pieces of coloured frescos and clay pots. It is a complex building, an agglomeration of rooms of Ist century A. D., enlarged until 2nd century A.D. with modifications until 4th century A. D.

The upper floor

(This give information about the well known pieces; the rooms are illustrate by explanatory cards).

Ist cella- There are prehistorical finds of bronze Age (about 1800 B.C.). In particular they are finds of Ancolithic period found in the famous Grotta della Tanaccia (Brisighella).

2nd cella- There are ceramics of different periods found in Ravenna.

3rd cella- There are finds of the excavations in the necropolis of St. Semero (Classe di Ravenna); boxes full of balsams, combs, keys, lanterns and what rests of Theodoric's cuirass found in Ravenna dockyard, only 100m. from Theodoric's Mausoleum.

4th cella- There are 5 archaistic and Hellenistic herms among which there is Miltiades' herm. They are fished out from the sea, offshore Porto Corsini (Po di Primaro);

they are part of a load sent by Cardinal Ippolito 2nd d'Este and sunk at the end of 1500.

At the end of the room there is a small marble sarcophagus of a baby, not belonging to Ravenna, dating back to the end of 3rd century A. D. On the front there is a figure with the unfinished face towards which a barefooted woman turns, and at the left extremities there is a boy with a dove in his hand.

5th cella- There are finds of the Roman necropolis of Classe (Palazzette) dating back to the Ist and 2nd century a. C.

6th cella- There is a bronze transenna made also with marble finely worked. There is a big cross removed from the dome of St. Vitale dating back to the 6th century; there is a piece of a mosaic representing the head of an angel, taken from a vault of the presbitery because it was slipping a century ago.

7th cella- On the right side there are 2 fragments of the lead pipes of the waterworks restored by the king Theodoric; the preservation

---

76 - *Funeral stele of the carpenter Publio Longidieno (I century).*
77 - *The deification of August, sculptural fragment of Parian marble of Claudia's time.*
78 - *Patera of the vanished Port'Aurea erected in A.D.*

80

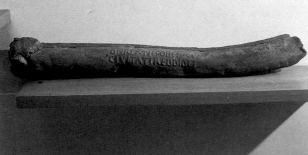

81

of this find which has a detailed stamping perfectly visible of king Theodoric, orderer of the work, is excellent.

8th cella- There are materials dating back to the 4th and 17th century.

9th cella- There are materials such as ivories and bones decorated with historical scenes. In the first case there is the "dittico di Murano" (Murano diptych), called in this way because it comes from the monastery of St. Michael in Murano. It is an evangeliary covering of Alexandrine school dating back to the 6th century. In the middle there is Christ while he is announcing the Word; at the sides there are some miracles (the recovery of the blind, of the paralytic and of the mad, and the Resurrection of Lazarus); in the lower part there is Jonah with the sea monster and the boys entering the furnace.

10th cella- ivories and pastorals.

11th cella- Furniture and grave goods.

12th-13th-14th cella- Ceramics dating back from 11th to 18th century.

We reach the **great hall** where the finds of the cemetery area under the Basilica of St. Apollinare in Classe, found in the last years, are situated.

66

82

83

On the right side there is the interesting Whole graphic project of apsidal bowl shaped vault of the same Basilica; after the removal of the mosaic by means of the mosaicists group of Ravenna, in order to be better preserved, this project of the Byzantine craftman's work of the 6th century has been found with a next intervention

---

79 - *Large sinopite in terra rossa found under the mosaic of St. Apollinare in Classe.*
80 - *Herma of Miltiades - Roman copy of Greek original of the middle of the V century B.C.*
81 - *Piece of lead pipes with the name of the King Theodoric perfectly preserved.*
82 - *St. Nicolas of Mira. Russian school.*
83 - *Mystical marriage of St. Catherine. School of Marches - XIV century.*
84 - *St. John of Damascus who receives the command by Christ. Slavic School - II century.*

84

85

technically successful, allowed the removal of the big sinopite made of red earth. The peacocks and the baskets not realized are well visible, they were substituted during the execution by some sheep.

On the left side there is an archeological curiosity, a proof of civil life dating back to the 2nd century A.D.; it is a memorial tablet found under the floor of the Basilica, sculpted on both sides, because it was reutilized.

86

85 - St. George and the Dragon - Creto-Venetian school - XVII-XVIII centuries.
86 - Virgin Odighitria - Creto-Venetian school XVI century.

On the left side there is a theory of Roman funerary steles of the «Classiarii» reutilized by the Christians, as the steles of the cloister at the ground floor, with the indication of origin, and of their ship.

On the front there are the names of the patrons of the *«matres»* and of the *«scribes»*, on the reverse there is the list of the smiths of the Roman fleet of Classe.

The icons room

A great number of Russian, Slavic icons and of Cretan and Venetian school, on which the Venetian influence on the particular artistic, religious and devotional expression of the last Byzantine painting is evident.

There are also the products of the local «contaminations» (of the Marches, Emilian an Bolognese etc.) sometimes gathered in groups of production to underline the serial work of these «painters of Madonnas».

The ceramics room

The exposition is divided in 4 parts. At the entrance there is the original nucleus of the museum of Classe, in which there are 2 interesting examples of Spanish-Moorish plates (Manise) of the 15th century, and an exhaustive but not wide panorama of the Italian production from 16th to 18th century (Deruta, Faenza, Forlì, Ravenna, Urbino).

Then, there are the beautiful examples of pharmaceutical vases (majolica jars, pill boxes, water-jugs, bottles etc.) of the 17th and 18th century of which the chemistries of the several monasteries were well-stocked in Ravenna.

At last there are the local «poor» productions found, for the great part, during the excavations near religious buildings (St. Agatha, new St. Apollinare, the Archbishop Palace) or near areas where old furnaces were situated (jugs, tankards, pots and dishes).

A very interesting didatic route ends the exposition. If you go out from the main gate, immediately turn left in «Via Galla Placidia» afte 10m. you reach the church of St. Maria Maggiore.

The church of St. Maria Maggiore

It was built by the bishop Ecclesio in the first quarter of the 6th century, it was rebuilt in 1671.

The previous building with a central plant was rebuilt with 3 aisles* and now, only the apse, the columns which bases have been raised with stones and capitals remain of the original building.

The big mosaic decoration with the image of the Madonna has disappeared. The bell-tower dates back to the 9th century. You reach the Church of Santa Croce (Holy Cross Church), going on only few metres.

The church of Santa Croce

It was built by Galla Placidia as a chapel or the Court because it is possible that the imperial Palace of Onorius and Galla Placidia was situated not far from here. It was shaped like a cross and decorated with precious marbles, and it was surely the most beautiful palace of the town. In its architectonical complex there was also the Mausoleum of Galla placidia, later built. The present apse, restored in these years after a big fire, is dating back to the 15th century, while the bell-tower is dating back to the 17th century.

Around the building 3.50m. under the ground there are pieces of beautiful polychrome floor mosaics, restored by the mosaicists group in 1978. The mosaics made of black and white marble in the outside are part of a Roman house built before the Church.

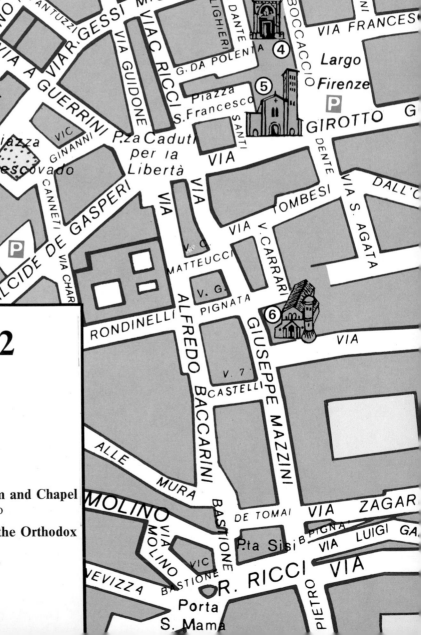

VIA GAB.

CAMILLO CAVOUR

VIA PAOLO COSTA

C. MORIGIA

PASOLINI

P.za
A. Costa

VIA

CASA MATHA

13 GIUGNO

ARIANI

VIA D.

ARMANDO D

⑪ ⑩

F. MORDANI

VIA ZIRARDINI

VIA GIUSEPPE

V. DI LONGHI

V. MAFALDA DI SAVOIA

G. MATTEOTTI

NOVEMBRE

Piazza
del Popolo

MURATORI

Piazza 20
Settembre

P.za L.
Einaudi

VIA G. ANTICA ZECCA

ARMANDO D

D'AZEGHO

9 FEBBRAIO

P.za
J. F.
Kennedy

VIA FANTUZZI

MENTANA

CAIROLI

Piazza G.
Garibaldi

VIA BOCCACCIO

VIA ANGELO MA

CORRADINI

VIC.

VIA FRANCES

G. GARATONI

VIA A GUERRINI

VIA GIOACCHINO RASPONI

VIA R. GESSI

VIA M. GORDINI

VIA C. RICCI

VIA GUIDONE

ALIGHIERI

V. DANTE

G. DA POLENTA

④

⑤

Largo
Firenze

GIROTTO G

Piazza
Duomo

VIA BATTISTERO

⑧

Piazza
Arcivescovado

VIC.
GINANNI

P.za Caduti
per la
Libertà

Piazza
S. Francesco

SANTI

VIA

DENTE

VIA S. AGATA

DALL'C

BIXIO

⑦

⑨

REA

CANNETI

ALCIDE DE GASPERI

VIA CHAR

VIA

MATTEUCCI

V. C.

VIA

V. CARRARI

TOMBESI

VIA S.

VIA S. TE

P

V. G.
PIGNATA

⑥

VIA

RONDINELLI

ALFREDO BACCARINI

V. 7

CASTELLI

GIUSEPPE MAZZINI

VIA

ALLE

MURA

BASTIONE

DE TOMAI

VIA ZAGAR

MOLINO

VIA MOLINO

Pta Sisi

B PIGNA

VIA LUIGI GA

VIA

NEVIZZA

VIC BASTIONE

R. RICCI

PIETRO

VIA

Porta
S. Mama

Itinerary n. 2

4 Tomb of Dante
Via Dante

5 Basilica of S. Francis
Piazza San Francesco

6 Basilica of S. Agatha
Via Mazzini

7 The Archbishop's museum and Chapel
Piazza Arcivescovado

8 Neonian Baptistry (or of the Orthodox or of the Cathedral)
Piazza Arcivescovado

9 Cathedral
Piazza Duomo

TOMB OF DANTE

(18th century)

87

Dante, during his life, took part in the suffering which ravaged Italy because of the intestine wars connected with the destiny of the rising European Powers; but also after the death, his bones had no peace.

He was guest of Guido Da Polenta in 1316; after having sadly wandered through Italy, he found little bit of peace here.

He made only few travels as ambassador of Guido Da Polenta; in this way he could finish the Divine Comedy comforted by his sons Beatrix, Jacopo and Peter. He died in the night between 13th and 14th September 1321, and after the funeral his body was placed in a sarcophagus near the church. The end of the domination of the family Da Polenta did not allow an adequate sepulchre to the poet; only in 1483, Pietro Lombardo, a ventian sculptor, (father of Tullio Lombardo which sculpted the Guidarello Guidarelli's statue) was charged by Bernardo Bembo, podesta of the Venetian Republic in Ravenna, to sculpt a bas-relief in honour of the Poet. The work which represents the poet reading, is visible in the wall in front of the sepulchre door. In 1780 Cardinal legate Luigi Valenti Gonzaga decided to build an adequate sepulchre giving the work to the architect of Ravenna Camillo Morigia, he built the present small temple in neo-classic style, keeping the part made by Lombardo. The people of Ravenna called ironically this building "la zucarira" that is to say the sugar-basin.

In 1921, 600 years after the death of the poet, the small temple was decorated covering with onyx the bare walls and utilizing rare marble for the finishing of the coating.

The bronze wreath under the bas-relief of Lombardo, was offered by the victorious army of the Ist World War.

The light hanging down from the dome, offered by the Dantesque society in 1908, is continuously fed with oil offered by Florence to Ravenna with a solemn rite on Sunday near September 14th every year; this is the day when the poet died.

There are the vicissitudes of Dante's mortal remains.

After Dante's death, the Florentines claimed the poet's mortal remains, but they never had them.

The risk that this compromise could take place, increased when Ravenna came back to the Papacy and 2 members of the family of Medici became

87 - *Tomb of Dante.*

71

popes, Leone 10th and Clemente 7th. Leone 10th because of a request allowed the Florentines to go to Ravenna and take Dante's mortal remains. Michelangelo in an annotation of this request said: "al divin Poeta fare la sepoltura nuova chondecente e in Lhoco onorevole in questa città". The Franciscan friars of the monastery nearby, through a hole in the adjacent wall and one in the sarcophaguses, filched the body and kept it hidden.

In 1677 the father Antonio Sarti made a recognition of the body which was put in a box with the indication «Dantis ossa demper revisa die Juni 1677».

The friars'attachment to the tomb and the body of a brother of them was so great that when in 1692 works of maintenance were indispensable to the tomb, an intervention of soldiers and of the police was necessary, these protected the workers. In 1810 the friars because of the Napoleonic laws had to leave the monastery and hid the box in a walled up door in the **Quadrarco of Braccioforte** (quadrangolar building with arches on each side). The box was refound by chance only 27th May 1865 during works of restoration of this building. Near the sepulcre in the garden full of laurel there is the Quadrarco di Braccioforte, an old oratory, restored after the works of 1865 in the 6th century of Dante Alighieri'birth. At the origin it was part of the narthex of the Basilica of St. Francis. The origin of the name goes back to a immage of Christ with the «estenso brachio» transalted in braccioforte. In this small garden, there are the remains of the wall where the box with the rests of the poet, found in 1865 was hidden in a walled up door: *2 monumental sarcophaguses* can be seen here: one is dated back to the end of 4th century, and belonging to the prophet Elisha and utilized by the old family from Ravenna Pignata. It is one of of the most important sculptures of Ravenna. On the front there is the Reedimer between Peter and Paul, who trample on the lion and the snake, symbols of the evil; on the back there are 2 deer which are watering and representing the catechumens while they are baptized; at both sides there are the doubtful visitation and the Annunciation.

The other sarcophagus dated back to the 6th century was utilized by the old family Traversari and has on the front a «tabula ansata» and on the acroters 2 peacocks; on both sides there is the Chrismon substained by 2 columns and the cross with the apocalyptic hanging letters alpha and omega.

In the yard there is the entrance of the **Dante town museum** where are displayed some relics, among which there is the box found by father Santi of which we have spoken at the beginning. **The library and the Dante medal and small bronze museum** have the entrance in Largo Firenze 9.

There are displayed manuscripts dated back to 1336, incunabula of the Divine Comedy and the Vernon code, dated back to the middle of 1300.

88

---

88 - *Monumental sarcophagus called «the Prophet Eliseo» (end of the IV century). On the front the Redeemer between St. Peter and St. Paul.*
89 - *Basilica of St. Francis.*

ST. FRANCIS

You can reach St. Francis square with the homonymic Basilica through a short avenue with cypresses and sarcophaguses made of calcareus rock dated back to the 5th and 6th century.

In front of it there is the wide portics of Province Palace and on the right there are the portics in Reinassance style built in 1936.

The basilica of St. Francis is dated back to the age of the bishop Neone in the middle of 5th century and it is dedicated to the Apostles; in fact the tomb of Neone was found here under the floor in the presbitery. The clay tubes of late Roman age of the original building, in particular of the apse, were found. Also here the mosaics which represent Peter and Paul have disappeared because the church was rebuilt and consecrated to St. Pier the Great about in 1000.

The old floor is 3,50m. under the ground. During the excavation in 1879, a tomb made of precious Greek marble and some rests of a wealthy golden diadem with pearls was found in this building; then, they were filched with the socalled Theodoric's cuirass from the National Museum.

In 17th and at the end of 18th century it was further damaged; thus, in 1700, there was the worst intervention when the original capitals were chiselled to be recovered with coloured stucco, the present ones are made of scagliola.

The present name dates back to 1261 when the archbishop Fontana gave it to the Franciscan Friars.

The narthex which embellished the façade has disappeared , only in the right side some traces have remained; in the part called Quadrarco di Braccioforte.

Only in 1921 (600 years after the death of Dante Alighieri) the church was restored and brought back its old shape. The importance of this church is due to Dante who knelt down and prayed here; his solemn funerals took place here in 1321 and nearby there is his sepulchre.

The quadrangular bell-tower, 32.90 metres high, which dates back to the 9th century is lightened by a two light window, a three* light window and with a late four light window. **The inside** is almost bleak, has 3 aisles with 24 columns made of Greek marble. They should be the remains of the Neptune temple (2 columns have pagan inscriptions); the pulvins are ancient while the capitals have been made skillfully (by Galassi of Ravenna) in scagliola from the impressions taken from 2 original capitals which have remained almost unaltered (Ist column on the right and on the left of the high altar).

The fourteenth century **cealing** is made of wood, shaped like a keel of an upset ship; has coloured squares and it was widely restored in 1921.

The mensa of the high altar is situated under an interesting sarcophagus dating back to the 4th century, belonging to the archbishop Liberius with 14 figures of the Apostles and Christ. It shows Eastern characteristics and precisely Byzantine.

The suggestive **crypt*** of the 10th century, always submerged by a wide water bed, has a floor mosaic with 2 mosaic Greek and Latin ephigraphs of multicoloured marble. It was restored in 1973 by the mosaicists group of Ravenna with new techniques. The inscription in Greek should have covered the original tomb of the bishop Neone. In the left aisle, near the high altar there is the Reinassance **urn** of Juffo Numai, humanist and secretary of Pino degli Ordelaffi, lord of Forlì, who died in 1509.

Near the exit there is the **land-slab** dating back to the 15th century of Enrico Alfieri, general minister of the Franciscan Order. Then, there is another land-slab of red Veronese marble; belongign to Ostasio da Polenta, with the face and the hands in white marble. Ostasio da Polenta died 14 March 1396. Then, there is a **sarcophaguses** dating back to the end of 4th century, with the lions feet, worked in high-relief.

On its front there are 5 shrines with spiral columns; in the central niche there is Christ in the position of the "*Traditio Legis*" on which St. Paul is recognizable; the tradition says that he has a wide balding at the temples. On this sarcophagus rise the painted arch of the chapel of Polentani (Polentani were lords of Ravenna from the end of 13th to the middle of 15th century). It was pratically demolished, only traces of frescos of 14th century school can be noted.

Nearby there is another pagan sarcophagus of the 3rd century with some puttos, it was reutilized as a tomb by the the patrician Del Sole, family of Ravenna; descendants of Guidarello Guidarelli immortalized by Tullio Lombardi; at the town pinacotheca there is the sepulcral statue of Guidarello in the Lombard loggia.

Near the exit on the left, fragments of sarcophaguses shaped like a niche of the beginning of the 6th century are fixed on the wall.

90

90 - *Central nave of the Basilica.*
91 - *Wonderful view of the crypt (X century).*
92 - *Suggestive view of the flooded crypt in its normal state.*

93

94

96

97

95

93 - Back side of the sarcophagus of Liberio III (end of the IV century) of the greater altar.

94 - Side of the sarcophagus of Liberio III of the greater altar (detail).

95 - Left side of the sarcophagus «of the niches» (end of the IV century) detail.

96 - Tomb-stone of Alfieri, General Minister of the Franciscans (XV century).

97 - Tomb-stone of Ostasio from Polenta (early 1400).

98 - 99 - Church of St. Agatha.

100 - 101 - Pieces of the original mosaics on the windows of the apse (VI century?).

THE CHURCH OF ST. AGATHA

(6th century)

It is difficult to establish what remains of the original building of the age of Julian the silversmith. The façade restored in 1918 has the corridor and the upper window with 2 lights of Renaissance age.

It was seriously damaged by the earthquake of 11th April 1688, the church still has the left wall out of lead so that the second and the 3rd columns are reinforced with 2 counterforts. The Allied bombardment of 1944 caused other damage to the apse and the left aisle.

The rebuilding, made in different ages, has an hybrid style as it can be seen in the 2nd column made with Greek and gray and cipollin granite with capitals of Roman, Byzantine and Renaissance age, recovered from disappeared monuments, while the original plan of the church is at 2.50m. depth.

However, the mobility of the building is evident seeing the original mosaics with olive leaves, in the splayed-jambs of the 5 window of the apse.

At the origins the mosaic of the 6th century covered all the apsidal bowl shaped-vault, it represents Christ sitting on the throne, on both sides there are 2 archangels on a golden background.

Between the 5th and 6th columns there is a pulpit with 3 aisles made of marble fluted with horizontal veins; it is thought that this pulpit was recovered from a big column; in the upper border there is a decoration with ovules and leaves of classic origins. The mensa is situated under a sarcophagus which contains the remains of the bishop Agnello (6th century) and the martyr

Sergio. At the entrance and outside remains of ancient heathen sarcophagi, later reutilized or not finished; they were found during the excavations at the end of 19th century and in 1914/18, in the area before the church where there was surely an arcaded court and an old cemetery.

We again find the sarcophagus, a typical sepulchre of Ravenna in ancient times. It is made of calcareous rock, used at the end of 5th until the beginning of 7th century for economic and practical reasons. It replaced the arches of Greek marble because of the high cost of the latter and it fell into disuse when the Slavs invaded Dalmatia and Forbade its importation.

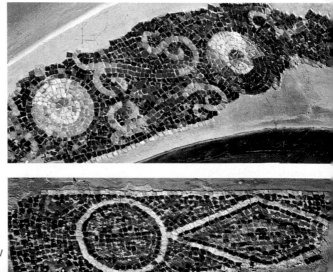

ARCHIEPISCOPAL MUSEUM AND CHAPEL

(6th century)

They are inserted in an agglomeration of buildings of different ages where the archbishop's palace is; they are blocks (for example the Roman Tower which bordered the Salustra Gate) which may be seen in the garden; and the first date back to the 5th century.

Archiepiscopal museum

The entrance of the museum and the archiepiscopal chapel ism in the part built in the 18th century. At the upper floor there is the archiepiscopal archives with a collection of papyrus and 13.000 parchments; some of these are dating back to the 8th century, and important documents of the story of the church of Ravenna. In the IST ROOM, in front of the entrance door, there are **pieces of mosaics** (the only remained) coming from the decoration ordered by the bishop Jeremy to substitute the previous mosaic in the Basilica Ursiana; The basilica Ursiana was built in 384 and demolished in 1734 by the architect Gianfranco Buonamici in order to have enough space to build the present cathedral: the central mosaics represent the praying Virgin Mary and on the left there are the heads of St. Peter St. John and of a soldier or a disciple and on the left there is St. Barbatian and St. Ursicino.

There are a lot of Christian and pagan inscriptions, capitals, plutea*, transennas, and funerary slabs; in front of the entrance between them there is a small christian Stele of a man called Antifonte, with a simple and rough pastoral image.

104

105

106

107

On the left wall, above, there is a marble slab shaped like a square. 19 sectors are sculpted on a circle: it is a **liturgic calendar** to calculate Easter for 94 years and exactly from 532 to 626. In that time it was normal to build a liturgic calendar to calculate Easter, which has a mobile date referring to the

102 - *Agglomeration of buildings of various periods (Cathedral, Oratory of St. Andrea Torre Salustra, and so on).*
Mosaic of the Basilica of Ursus
103 - *The praying Madonna (XII century).*
104 - *St. Peter (XII century).*
105 - *St. John (XII century).*
106 - *St. Barbatian (XII century).*
107 - *St. Ursicinus (XII century).*
108 - *Liturgical calendar of the Easter for the years 532-626.*

108

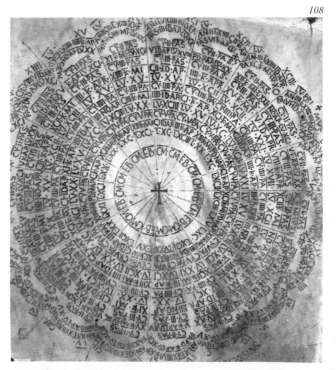

Hebraic calendar. The mortal remains of St. Quirico and St. Juliet are in **the Host receptacle** with their names; on the front there is a scene of the Three Kings adoration and on the back with a scene of the Traditio Legis.

In the RIGHT ROOM, there is a solid headless statue made of porphyry; traditionally it is thought that the statue represented Justinian or an imperial member, but it was really built in 4th or 5th century, thus it is much older.

Near the entrance door there is the marble **ambo***, coming from the church of St. John and Paul; it recalls the decoration of the pulpit in the cathedral of the bishop Agnello, even if it is smaller and built after the ambo in the cathedral.

In the ROOM NEARBY, in a wide display there is **the chasuble** of Rinaldo da Correggio (14th century) and in another display there is the very interesting chasuble* of St. John Angeloptes, with a doubtful execution (10th or 12th century,) it is red with a golden board finely embroidered, dotted with eagles and golden halfmoons.

The much interesting work is in the room nearby. It is the beautiful **ivory desk*** of the monogram sculpted in the bench says: «Maximianus Episcopus»; probably it is a generous gift of the Emperor Justinian. Under this work there are 5 slabs which have in the middle St. John Baptist on the 4 Evangelists in different positions of clear classic origin and deeply worked almost in full relief. Inside and outside the bench 12 episodes of Christ's life are represented; on the side there are 10 panels, 5 on each part representing the story of Joseph the Jew. This is surrounded with transverse and vertical strips rich of vaults of plants, lions, deer and peacocks and of a clear Eastern taste. The authors are a lot and the best pictures seem those in the bench.

The execution could be of the Alexandrian school dating back to the 6th century or of Egyptian school at the same period. Some slabs were found in many cities in Italy at the end of the last century and at the beginning of this one. They were restored by the Central institut of History in Rome in 1956. The missing parts were covered with a lightly pokerworked parchment in order to give a sign of reading.

---

109 - *Marble Host-receptacle of the saints Quirico and Judith with the Three Kings (on the front).*

110 - *Ivory throne of the Archbishop Maximian (VI century).*

109

110 ▶

111 - Detail of the throne: St. John Baptist in the middle and the four Evangelists on both sides; high the monogram of the Archbishop.

112 - Detail of the throne: multiplication of the loaves.

113 - Vestibule of the chapel: the Redeemer who tramples on the serpent and the lion.

82

The Archiepiscopal chapel

This was erected by Bishop Peter II as a private chapel for the bishops of Ravenna and then dedicated by Maximian to St. Andrew, the Apostle of Constantinople. The period of its building coincides with the reign of Theodoric and thus with the decline of catholic buildings.

Some parts of the original mosaic decoration have been lost. The last important rinnovation dates back to the beginning of the century, when it took on its present form with the apse being completely rebuilt.

It is a small building made up of two distinct parts: a vestibule with a barrel-shaped vault and a sacellum shaped like a Greek cross and a very small apsidal cell.

The barrel-shaped vault of the vestibule is decorated with birds and lilies, while in the tympanum of the entrance hall there is a representation of a pagan triumph of the Warrior Christ with a halo, cuirass, regal mantle and cross, in the act of trampling on a serpent and the head of a lion, symbols of the powers of evil; he holds a book in his hands where one reads in Latin *«Io sono la via, la verità e la vita»* which means: *«I am the way, the truth and the life»*.

Only the upper part is original, because the lower one has been distempered (recent-checks have revealed the cuirass), imitating the mosaic-material at the beginning of the century, when another distemper-decoration, which depicted Christ wearing a tunic, was eliminated.

The two lateral walls have exameter winds, famous because they are used to display at their best the main feature of the mosaic, which is the unique way in which it reflects all the light falling on it *«Aut lux hic nata est aut capta hic libera regnant.....»*, which means: *«Either the light begins here or once imprisoned, it reigns freely»*.

Almost all the inscription has been distempered according to the text handed down by the historian Andrea Agnello's pontifical Book about the Church of Ravenna (IX century).

The reconstruction, however, which has taken place on the basis of the discoveries made in 1911, is not only formal, but it has also the aim not interrupting the decoration of the barrel-shaped roof of which it is an integral part.

The chapel, shaped like a Greek cross, has a cross-shaped roof with a gold background, in which the clipeus* stands out in the centre with the monogrammatic transcription of the name of Jesus Christ with the Greek initials I and X.

The Clipeus is held up by four angels

with their hands out-stretched towards Christ, with the four Evangelists in between with their Gospels. The angel's harshness reminds us of the period of Theodoric, while the four Evangelists'symbols are not displayed as in the style of Galla Placidia with zoomorphic-forms but are instead complete with halos and books.

The apse was rebuilt between 1914 and 1920, originally using a structure of clay pipes. Its design was based on the original decoration, a few vague traces of which had remained.

The lateral lunettes, originally mosaical, were painted in fresco by Luca Longhi of Ravenna (at the end of the 16th century) with scenes of the «Deposition» and the «Ascension». The most interesting parts are in the four undersides of the arches: two of these have medallions of the six Apostles on each side, separated in the centre by a bust of Christ haloed and young, and the other two with the six Saints with big eyes, white veils and flowers in their hair. In the centre of the latter there is a medallion with the monogram of Christ with Alpha and Omega which symbolize the existential arch of Man.

The medallions on the right, e.g. Policarpo, Cosma and Damiano, are distempered and have no connection with the decoration.

Having concluded the exam of the mosaics, we see on the left a big silver Byzantine cross (VI century), which is an embossed work.

118

114 - *The Chapel.*
115 - *Detail of the under arch: the Redeemer.*
116 - *Detail of the under arch: an Apostle.*
117 - *Three Saints of the under arch.*
118 - *The four angels, alternated with the symbols of the four Evangelists, carry the monogram of Jesus Christ.*

This is the cross donated by the Bishop Agnello to the Basilica Ursiana. In the centre there is the Resurrection and on the back the praying Virgin, remade in 1559, while on the wings there are five medallions on each side with figures of Saints.

85

THE NEONIAN OR ORTHODOX BAPTISTRY (OR THE BAPTISTRY OF THE CATHEDRAL)

(5th century)

At a few metres from the Archbishop's Museum and beside the Cathedral there is the Baptistry of Neoniano named «Orthodox» in order to distinguish it from the Arian one, built 50 years later, at the time of the Arian Ostrogothic king, Theodoric. It is the most ancient remaining monument of Ravenna, maybe partly built on a Roman bath. Bishop Ursus who is thought to have died between the end of the 4th and the begin of the 5th century, erected a new Baptistry on it for his great Basilica (destroyed in 1734 in order to build the present Cathedral).

The Baptistry was certainly connected with the Basilica, through an annular ambulatory and other buildings such as the «catechumenium», the «consignatorium», and the «vestiarium», which are the rooms where baptisms were held. Here the undressed catechumens washed and were anointed; then there was the baptism with the immersion in the baptismal bath repeated three times after having rejected Satan and having been exorcized.

But at the end of the 5th century Bishop Neone finished the building and probably he added the dome in place of the lacunar; this addition was made using different types of brick and the primitive plaster goes beyond the impost of the dome, which in the lower part is made of clay pipes put one inside the other, while the upper part is made of Vesuvian pumice-stone.

Moreover Neone ordered the decoration of the dome with the present mosaics.

The primitive floor is 3 metres below; consequently the outside doors in the four apsidioles projecting from the building are no longer visible.

Thus it is clear that the proportions are altered and distorted today; in particular inside, the upper trampling plain takes away a great deal of the architectural energy of the building and the mosaic-decoration.

The discharging arches alternated with the extradosses of the 4 niches, are visible from the ground level; higher up there are windows with round arches and two pilaster strips for each side of the octagon. It is important to embrace that the building of the baptistries with an octagonal-form (which is also typical of the Ambrosian Baptistries) is not accidental or just of aesthetic origin; the symbolic reference is to the 7 days of the creation of the World and to the 8th day, that is the day of the Resurrection and Eternal Life, too.

Interior

The mosaic of the central part of the **dome** portrays St. John the Baptist who

119

119 - Neonian Baptistry.
120 - Original stuccos with figure of the Prophets.
121 - On pages 88-89: partial view of the interior.

baptizes Christ standing in the waters of the Jordan according to the inscription. John the Baptist is personified by an old pagan man who holds in one hand a garment to dry Christ and in the other one a reed. The composition of the water, which covers veil-like the submerged part of Christ, is very interesting.

One must note here the part which has been rebuilt during the middle of the last century, by the Roman Felice Kibel.

Once again this inexpert restorer has introduced completely wrong iconographic motifs. It is completely invented the «patera» with which St. John the Baptist pours the lustral water over the head of Christ.

In the primitive mosaic St. John the Baptist put his hand on Christ's head as in many normal Baptism involving total immersion in water and as one sees in the same scene in the Arian Baptistry. The bejewelled cross was also added at an unknown date.

On the **floor immediately below**, the Church is personified by the twelve Apostles.

They can be identified by reading their names which are written alongside each head; their hands, covered by veils, following a liturgical rite, hold crowns, symbolizing the idea of martyrdom.

The movement of the Apostles' theory has a solemn effect in its ceremonies in which the procession, starting from two opposite directions, meets Peter and Paul.

The approach of clear Roman classic influence is not different from the mosaics of Gallia Placidia, even if maybe of an earlier date; the procession reminds us of the triumphal cycles of the imperial epoch, but there the saints glorify the triumph of the Saviour.

Very high leaves of acanthus, like gigantic candlesticks, heighten the intermediate spaces while the rhythmic dynamism of the procession is brought out by the varied clothing of the Apos-

tles at one moment dressed in a golden tunic, the next in a white pallium.

The successive decoration with rich illusory structures which remind us of the Pompeiian frescos is divided among 8 ciboriums or small altars with pluteris and transennas which present alternately the 4 gospels and the throne.

In addition to the throne, in itself symbol of sovereignity, there is also the Christian completion of Christ' Cross with an allusion to the Apocalypse.

The 8 lunettes, in which the windows are opened, have the upper part decorated with stuccos of the 5th century, which were erased at the end of the last century, but remade with a neutral colour. It is a great mistake to consider these stuccos as additions of the 17th century. It was this opinion which allowed such a destructive intervention.

On the contrary to the right and to the left of the windows there are the remaining original stuccos; they are niches of the Old Testament prophets with a Laticlave tunic and pallium.

Over the tympanum of the same niches there are many scenes of the Old Testament: Daniel in the lions, Christ and St. Paul in a scene of *«Traditio*

124 - *St. John who baptizes Christ (detail).*

125 - *Detail of the head of St. Peter.*

126 - *Arabesque with festoon of acanthus and one prophet.*

Legis», Christ who tramples on the serpent and the lion, Jonah.

These works, ignored by the critics, represent, however, a product of the best quality and coherence with the rest of the building, considering that those were painted, too.

The arches below, which stand on 8 columns with capitals of Corinthian and Ital-Byzantine style have an arabesque mosaic of acanthus leaves, remade at the beginning of the century. Three of the four niches, now bare, have some monograms, interpreted in different ways.

Particularly the monogram to the west interpreted Maximian. The name of the Archbishop Maximian makes us think that he took part in some works in some ways and perhaps in the mosaic-decoration of the niches themselves, which explains the didascalic part of the inscriptions (restored and integrated but not entirely rebuilt).

The beatiful decorations of marble inlaying of porphyry, «pavonazzetto», (which is a type of a whitish marble with violet veins) serpentine and white marbles, complete the colouring of the interior.

In the centre of the Baptistry the octagonal Baptismal bath for the baptisms involving emersion, as explained at the beginning, rebuilt and recovered with slabs of Greek marble and porphyry is of extreme semplicity. The Baptisms took place in the Greek marble pulpit (end of the V century).

91

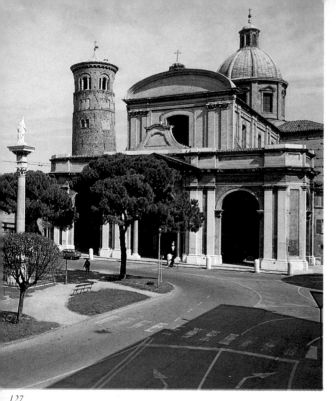

127

THE CATHEDRAL

(18th century)

It was built by the architect Gianfrancesco Buonamici of Rimini, in 1737, in place of the ancient cathedral* with a nave and four aisles dedicated to the Resurrection and built by Bishop Neone in the first years of the 5th century. This building is very interesting to talk about, because it was the first great church built inside the walls of the town.

The move of the Imperial Court from Milan to Ravenna made it advisable to take the Bishop from Classe to Ravenna, and build a Cathedral worthy of the event. Then the Basilica of Ursus was rebuilt between the 9th and the 10th century.

When later the architect Buonamici put his hand on it, he carefully designed the mosaics of the apse dated 1112 and carried out, fotlowing Archbishop Geremia's orders in agreement with Archbishop Farsetti, everything possible to hasten the construction of a new Cathedral.

92

The remains of the original Cathedral are in the external central portico. They consist of two columns of pink granite and two columns of Greek marble of the principal door and the cript, discovered by chance in 1864, dating back to the 10th century. The bell-tower, built in three different periods dates back to the tenth century.

It is built on the Latin Cross plan with a nave and two aisles with twelwe columns on each side, rich in valuable marbles, sculptured, frescos and paintings above all of the 17th and the 18th centuries.

The oval dome, originally octagonal, is a work of the architect Giuseppe Pistocchi of Faenza (1780).

In the transept on the left the Chapel of the Most Holy Sacrament (among others things) decorated with frescos of Guido Reni (1620) and the chapel on the right named after Madonna of the Sweat with paintings of Andrea and Giambattista Barbiani (1656) are worthy of particular attention.

In this last chapel, in both niches, there are exceptional examples of Christian* sarcophaguses of the 5th century.

On the right there is the sarcophagus of the Barbaziano coming away from

129

tion of Ravenna. While the Roman sar-cophagi are carved only on three sides because they are destined to be leaning against the wall and with flat lids, those of Ravenna are modelled on four sides and with a weathered lid or in the shape of a barrel due to an evident influence derived from the regular contact between Ravenna and the East, particularly Egypt and Syria.

The sarcophagi of Ravenna,

130

the beatiful but destroyed (1553) Basilica of St. Lawrence in Caesarea. St. Barbaziano, a Syrian, was a doctor, confessor and friend of Galla Placidia for about 20 years.

The sarcophagus presents on the front 5 niches with Christ in the centre and alongside St. Peter and St. Paul, in high-relief.

On the round lid there is a crown with the monogram of Christ, in the centre, usually considered a decadent work, but which should be considered on the contrary as harmonious, meaningful and uniform, even if it seems a little bit baroque in its thousand decorations.

On the left one can see the sarcophagus in which the remains of St. Ronald from Concoreggio were put in 1321 and which portrays on the front a scene of the *«Traditio Legis»* with Christ sitting on a mountain, from which the four symbolic rivers flow in the act of receiving St. Peter and St. Paul.

One can be allowed to linger near the sarcophagi, because they represent in the ancient sculpture an original tradi-

131

---

127 - *The Cathedral.*
128 - *The Chapel of the Holy Sacrament with a painting of Reni.*
129 - *Sarcophagus of St. Barbatian (V century).*
130 - *Detail of the «Traditio Legis» of the sarcophagus of the St. Rinaldo (V century).*
131 - *The ambo of the Bishop Agnello (VI century).*

93

ET · MAXIMIANI · AB · ECCI · S · ANDREA

ARA · RECOND · VIII · KAL · AVG · MDCCCIX ·

132 - 133 - Details of the sarcophagus of Esusperantio and Maximian (V century).   132

which are the umbilical cord between ancient and pre-romanic sculptures are a separate thing both for their forms and their artistic unity.

Under the third arch of the central nave, we can see the Greek marble pulpit (6th century), reconstructed in the present position in 1913, from the ancient Basilica of Ursus, built by the Bishop Agnello, maybe (but we consider it unlikely) from two lids of monumental sarcophaguses. It is tower-shaped, decorated in fishes, peacocks, ducks, lambs, deers and doves; this ambo of simple construction takes on great importance, because we know its date for certain given by the carved inscription which says: Bishop Agnello *«pyrgum fecit»*. Going on towards the exit, the third altar on the right nave has the altar-frontal formed by a sarcophagus of the first half of the 15th century coming from the lost Church of S. Agnes. It holds the mortal remains of Bishop Esusperanzio and in 1909 also the remains of the Bishop Maximian were added.

On the front there is Christ with St. Peter and alongside St. Paul with two palms. This is the last sarcophagus of Ravenna with human figures: after there came images with architectural decorations and symbolic subjects, but the marble will go on to be imported from the distant isle Marmora, to give us other marvellous examples of sculpture.

94

· EXVPERANTII · AB

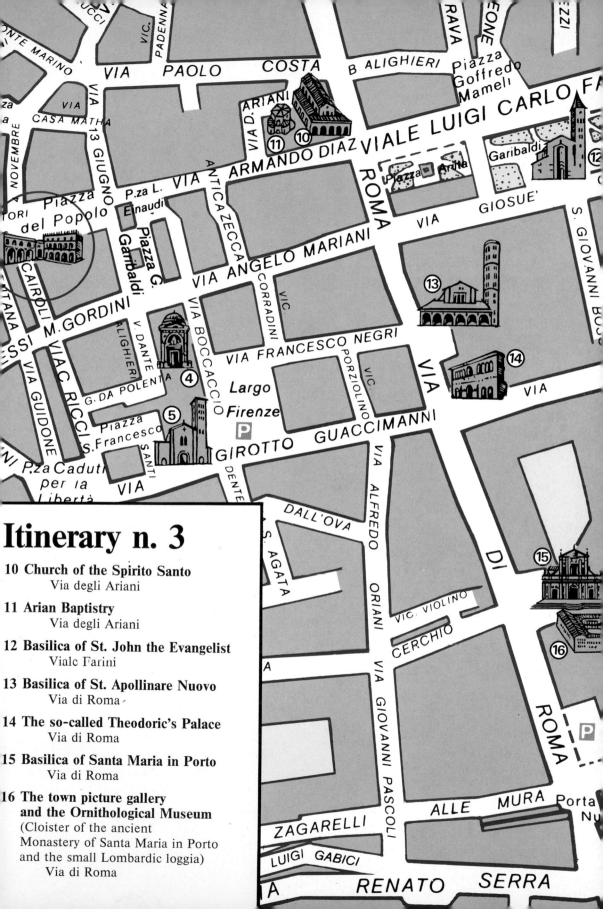

Itinerary n. 3

10 Church of the Spirito Santo
Via degli Ariani

11 Arian Baptistry
Via degli Ariani

12 Basilica of St. John the Evangelist
Viale Farini

13 Basilica of St. Apollinare Nuovo
Via di Roma

14 The so-called Theodoric's Palace
Via di Roma

15 Basilica of Santa Maria in Porto
Via di Roma

**16 The town picture gallery
and the Ornithological Museum**
(Cloister of the ancient
Monastery of Santa Maria in Porto
and the small Lombardic loggia)
Via di Roma

134

THE CHURCH OF SPIRITO SANTO
(6th century)

Ancient Cathedral of the Arian cult, built at the beginning of the 6th century, by Theodoric, was originally dedicated to the *Hagia Anastasis* that is the Resurrection of God: this dedication must not amaze us, because it is to be stressed that the links between Greece and Ravenna were very strong for centuries. As for the Arian Baptistry added shortly after Theodoric's death (526), this was consacrated by Bishop Agnello to the Catholic cult and dedicated to St. Teodoro, soldier and martyr of Amasea in Ponto. The external Renaissance portico was built in 1543 the occasion of the partial rebuilding of the Church, using three spiral semi-columns of Greek marble which supported the ancient canopy of the altar of the Church.

Little remains of the original Cathedral: there is the greater nave, the apse, and the triumphal arch and the 14 columns (13 of grey marble and one of cipolin) with capitals and original Theodoric pulvins with cross and disc.

In the apse traces of frescos with the St. Theodor's life; have been found therefore it is possible to imagine that eventual mosaic decorations have had a very short life; on the contrary it is likely that at the moment of the consacration Bishop Agnello had made a purging in the Basilica of St. Apollinare Nuovo.

The ambo of the middle of the 6th century presents on the front three chilled aediculas with cantharus*, vines and grapes.

Legend says that the final name of the Church of Spirito Santo is due to the fact that the bishops were elected by a dove (the Spirito Santo) which went among the Christians who were gathered praying in its Church; the name «Dove Bishop» came about in this way.

The painting of Lino Agresti of thc 16th century shows this legend.

In the south side of the Church there is a wall of the socalled **HOUSE OF DROGDONE OR DROEDONE**, considered the remains of the buildings of the Arian Bishop's episcopate, but certainly it is more recent, in fact it can be considered late Byzantine.

---

134 - *Church of the Holy Spirit.*
135 - *Central nave and apse.*
136 - *The wall of the House of Drogdone.*

135

136

THE ARIAN BAPTISTRY
(6th century)

A short distance from the Church of the Spirito Santo there is the Arian Baptistry, built by the Arian gothic king Theodoric between the end of the 5th century and the beginning of the 6th century, and almost contemporary with the building of the Basilica of S. Apollinare Nuovo.

Later in 565, after the condamnation of the Arian Church and its destruction it was adapted as an oratory of the catholic cult with the name of St. Maria following an imperial edict.

The basilian monks, coming from Greece built a monastery here during the exarchal period, adding to Santa Maria the name «Cosmedin» becoming in this way «S. Maria in Cosmedin». In 1667 a building for oratorial use was added to it; in 1700 it passed into the hands of private citizens, until 1914 when it was bought by the Italian State. Then it began a long legal fight to liberate the building from all the structures that for centuries had been added to it. Only the bombardment of 1943 and 1944 (it is hard to admit it) gave a decisive blow, revealing its real structures or at least whatever remained of it.

Like the Baptistry of the Cathedral and other monuments of Ravenna, it was underground; as a matter of fact the original floor is 2.30 metres above the road. On the left we can see the beginning of the wall of the ambulatory in the shape of a vault which ran around the baptistry.

It is octagonal in shape with four great niches; in the mosaic-decoration of the dome we can again note the theme of the Neonian Baptistry that is the Baptism of Christ by St. John.

The fact that the Baptistry repeats both the architectural scheme and the decorative one of the Orthodox Baptistry, means that at least at the beginning there was no antagonism between the two churches; it reflected Theodoric's initial ideas. Also here the Baptism involved immersion in water; the priest put his right hand on the Catechumen's head to persuade him with a gentle push to su bmerge himself three times.

The mosaic

So Christ is baptised by St. John while the dove of the Spirito Santo, according to the thesis, sprays lustral water from its beak or emanates the Spirito Santo; half of Christ is submerged in the Jordan's water, where he is shown as an old man with a leather bag beside, from which the water flows out, and two chelae of crab on his head,

---

137 - Arian Baptistry.

139

138 - Decoration of the wall.
139 - Christ receives the Baptism by John.
140 - St. Peter (detail).

99

◄138

140

141

142

which is a typical attribute of the sea and river-gods.

In the part below, the procession of the Apostles is going towards the cruciferous throne, symbol of God's sovereignity, confirmed by a bejewelled cross, on a splendid purple cushion, placed on the throne.

We can remember that the throne replaced the figured image of the Emperor and in the Christian symbology, Christ.

Trunks of date-palms, rich in fruits, gifts of the martyrs for the sacred acts which they have done, divide the Apostles' figures; ten of them curry the crown of the martyrdom and the glory, with veiled hands in the mystic and liturgic rite. St. Peter, on the right of the throne, carries the keys of Paradise and St. Paul, in his usual baldness, on the left, carries two volumes. His clothing and footwear are typically Roman.

Looking closely one can see the stylistic and technical difference with which the mosaic decoration has been made including between the second palm on the left and the first on the right of the throne and regarding the figures of St. Peter (with his clothing of white marble and not of glass paste), St. Paul, St. Thomas, the central medaillon, compared to the remaining 9 Apostles. The First part expresses the Roman classical influence with flatter figures. The Roman restorer Kibel invented a stucco brew of cooked oil.

There are no traces of the marbles, stuccos and mosaics, in comparison with the Cathedral Baptistry; in the excavations carried out, more than 170 kilos of tesseras were found under the floor; this shows that the decoration should be more wide-spread than today.

---

141 - *The throne with bejewelled cross and purple cushion.*

142 - *Mosaic decoration (detail).*

143 - *Basilica of St. John the Evangelist.*

THE BASILICA OF ST. JOHN THE EVANGELIST

(5th century)

143

It is situated at the edge of an ancient necropolis of the Ist century A.D. where in 1965 many graves of people, who had been cremated, were found.

The Church was partly reerected in the post-war period, after the severe damage caused by the Anglo-American bombardments; the damage was so great, that at a certain point the idea of demolishing everything was considered as it was done for the other ancient Church of St. Vittore in Ravenna.

The Basilica of St. John the Evangelist is the most ancient in Ravenna. The gothic portal* (14th century) with its bas-reliefs tells us about the origins of this building.

Galla Placidia, exiled to Constantinople, came back to Ravenna in 424 in order to take possession of the Empire for her son Valentinian III who was going to assume government.

The ship which carried them, was hit by a storm in the Aegean Sea in sight of the sanctuary of the Saint of Ephesus and Gallia Placidia vowed to erect a church to St. John the Fisherman, if she was saved.

The ship succeeded in berthing and after some years a magnificent basilica rich in splendid mosaics, was erected in the area of imperial Ravenna.

Apart from the legend, its building had the political meaning of the supremacy of the descendants of Theodosius over Honorius' party. In the spire of the portal there is Christ, St. John Evangelist, Gallia Placidia, her son Valentinian III priest and the friend and confessor S. Barbaziano of Antioch, whose monumental sarcophagus is in the chapel of the Virgin of the Sweat of the Cathedral. The legend, which illustrated in the lower part in the portal, arose because the Basilica didn't have any relics of the Saint.

Galla Placidia was very unhappy about the lack of any Saint's relic for the church, which she had built. In the night, however, St. John appeared to Galla Placidia and left to both St. Barbaziano and Galla Placidia a pontifical sandal.

The Church, which suffered several rebuildings also in the medioeval period (among them the exceptionally high pronaos under which there is the entrance), was rebuilt for the last time in 1921.

Originally the Church should have been shorter than the present one,

101

144

because one can see the total narthex of which the walled arches on the left and on the right as soon as one enters. The portal was re-erected only in 1960, after the severe damage, we have spoken of at the beginning.

The square **bell-tower**, 42 metres high, is of the X century; its bells, Marzia and Dolorosa, were built by the famous founder Roberto Sassone.

The lagered spire has been recovered by white and green enamelled bricks. On one side of the bell-tower is the façade of the church: the bell-tower interior leans on a great granite column with a 5th century capital.

Here, as in all the ancient Basilicas of Ravenna, the original floor is necessary below the present one. The raising of the floor by about 2.80 metres above the original floor was necessary because despite the thick formations originally built on the particularly swampy ground, the problem of subsidence still remains.

The lifting up of the grey marble columns to the present floor destroys the architectural energy of the arches, reducing the beauty of the wall in the central nave. Only the two comumns of the triumphal arch on both sides of the apse are on the original floor. Nevertheless St. John Evangelist remains an excellent axample of early Christian architecture.

Unfortunately the mosaics were completely destroyed by the abbot Teseo Aldrovandi in 1568, owing to the cult of

«destructive renewal», which is typical in man'shistory.

The mosaic-decoration recounted the legend which is still described in the entrance: St. John's ship, the storm, Galla Placidia's family including her daughter Giusta Grata Onoria who was expelled from Court, because she was involved in scandal with the Court's butler.

The pulvins are the original ones of the Basilica of Gallia Placidia.

The ceiling, with its wooden beams (still visible) and trusses*, dates back to the XVI century even though it has been very restored.

In the aisle on the left, in the gothic style chapel there are traces of frescos of the Giottesque School of Rimini of the XIV century with a representation of the 4 Evangelists and the Doctors of the Church.

The fragments of **mosaics** with a popular subject, arranged on the same aisle's wall come from the medieval floor found at 1.75 metres and built by order of the Abbot Guglielmo in 1273. This medieval floor is the most ancient flooring.

From the entrance on the left there are scenes or the 4th Crusade, the taking of Zara and Constantinople; behind the gothic-style chapel there is a series of images showing fishes, dogs and ducks. In particular there is the story of a fox's funeral in which two corks carry the fox (hanging chained down), followed by a duck with a thurible. The fox wakes up and astonished the naive people, as in Aesop's famous moralistic fables.

The mosaics are made with semplicity and poor materials with large interstices.

Moreover the use of tesseras of glass paste (in particular various shades of turquoise) gives the impression of the use of salvage, maybe the original dating back to Galla Placidia's time.

Passing in front of the 5th century altar, we can see that it is composed of a

145

146

147

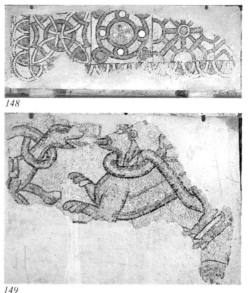

148

149

mensa and four pillars with a little door in front.

The diaconicon has an interesting small altar with pillars built at the end of the 6th century: in the front there is the image of a door between two spiral columns.

On both sides of the diaconicon's door there are two slabs, with pieces of mosaic of the 6th century with geometrical motifs which represent, together with the marble marquetry the most ancient layer, certainly dating back to the most ancient flooring.

Along the same wall there are other medieval mosaics and intermediate floors, with geometrical motifs and fantastic animals.

On the entrance door there is a very large painting of Carlo Bonone of Ferrore (1610) regarding the theme: «The feast of Ahasuerus».

---

144 - *Detail of the Portal of the XIV century with the legend of the sandal.*
145 - 146 - 147 - *Floor mosaics on the wall of the left nave (1273): Episodes of the 4th Crusade and the Constantinople and the fox' funeral.*
148 - 149 - *Floor mosaics on the wall of the right nave (X-XI century): decorative motifs and fantastic animals.*

150

THE BASILICA OF S. APOLLINARE NUOVO

(6th century)

This was erected by the Arians and dedicated to Jesus Christ by the king of the Goths, Theodoric, in the first quarter of the VI century.

Then this was reconsacrated by the Bishop Agnello to the catholic cult in 561 with the name of St. Martin in golden Heaven (St. Martin, Bishop of Tours, was also in implacable foe of heretics); probably this name originates both from the great quantity of the gold here and from the richly decorated ceiling.

Legend tells us about this subject, Pope Gregory the Great ordered the mosaics to be blackened because their brightness and their sparkling images distructed the Christians during the services.

The Basilica, although still beatiful, was certainly richer in mosaics, marbles and valuable metals, considering the nearness of the Real Palace and its function as Palatine Chapel.

Only with the removal, towards the middle of the XI century (maybe in 856) of the bones of the first Bishop of Ravenna, St. Apollinaris, from the Basilica of Classe, to Ravenna, in order to get away from the raids of the slavic pirates was it named St. Apollinare Nuovo.

The removal of the Saint's bones from Classe to Ravenna, gave rise to some controversy because the monks of Classe and those of Camaldoli, stated that the bones were in S. Apollinare in Classe, while the Benedectines replied that the relics had been definetly put in their Basilica of S. Apollinare Nuovo. It was necessary for the Pope Alexander III who sended a legacy in order to clarify the situation and restore peace. The legacy, following precise surveys, decided that the bones were in Classe.

The pronaos (a small portico supported by some columns in the front of the church) and the mullioned window with two lights above are Renaissance, reconstructed after the damage of the first World War: on the 12th of February 1916 an Austrian bomb destroyed the portico and produced a large hole in the upper part in the left of the façade.

150 - *Basilica of S. Apollinare Nuovo.*
151 - *Interior: central nave.*
152 - *On pages 106-107: general view of the left wall.*

The beautiful round and 38.50-metre-high bell-tower lightened by three mullioned windows with one light, three mullioned windows with three lights, dates back to the beginning of the XI century.

The harmonic and simple interior has three naves divided by 12 columns on each side (the 12 Apostles) made of Greek marbles with Corinthian capitals and dosserets with crosses. Even here, as in the nearby St. John the Evangelist, the floor has been raised above the original; therefore the columns have been lifted up above the floor which spoils the beauty of the arches.

This operation dates back to the years 1514/1520.

Regarding that period, it can be described as audacious even if it is likely that this operation helped the walls of the central nave to fall down and so a great deal of work was necessary to restore them.

In the bases there are simple faded and also Renaissance frescos with figures of saints.

The mosaic-decoration is the only one that has remained; the mosaic of the apse ordered by the Archbishop Agnello, was destroyed by the earthquake of the VIII century, while a piece of mosaic modified and attributed to the Emperor Justinian, is what has remained of the wall of the front door.

As a matter of fact it is likely that Justinian has a great importance in the iconography of the mosaic-decoration in place of the one which portrays Theodoric and his Court. Justinian leaving the new Basilica to Agnello, gave him unlimited powers in order to eliminate all the images which contrasted with the official religion of the Empire.

The left wall of the central nave

In the upper part, near the ceiling, alternating with decorative motifs representing the cross, two doves and a shell-shaped niche there are 13 small pictures which portray the tapestries for their irregular frames with scenes of Christ's Miracles and Parables.

They are of Theodoric's time, typical of the early Christian iconography, with a Christ who is young and curly, beardless with the imperial tunic of purple and pallium and the halo made of crossed shaped jewels.

Beginning from the front door, we can see:

1)The paralyzed Man of Bethesda now cured, carrying his bed (this was destroyed by the Austrian bomb and rebuilt on the basis of accurate designs); 2) The Healing of the man possessed by a devil (the evil spirits are represented by three pigs in the act of escaping); 3) The paralyzed Man of Capernaum is let down through the open roof in the house where Jesus is a guest; 4) Jesus as judge divides the sheep from the kids, that is the Last Judgement (on His right there are the lambs, on His left are the sinners represented by spotted kids); 5) The poor widow Mite; 6) The Pharisee prays with his lifted arms and the Publican beats his breast in front of the Temple; 7) The Raising of Lazarus; 8) The Samaritan Woman at the well; 9) Christ indicated the scribes to the adulteress; 10) The Healing of the Blind Men at Jericho; 11) The Call where Peter and Andrew leave their nets to follow Christ; 12) The Miracle of the Loaves and the Fishes; 13) The Marriage at Cana (a work of a Roman restorer Kibel who instead of the transformation of the water into the wine, reproduced the miracle of the loaves); it is to be noted that the restored part is the inferior one and the kneeling young man is in profile in contrast with the rule of the frontality of the other figures of the entire cycle.

108

153

153 - *Decoration of the upper part (shell-shaped motif) of Theodoric'time.*

Small pictures with scenes of miracles parable of Christ:

154 - *St. Peter and St. Andrew leave the nets to follow Christ.*

155 - *Lazarus' resurrection (detail).*

156 - *Jesus, as judge divides the lambs from the kids.*

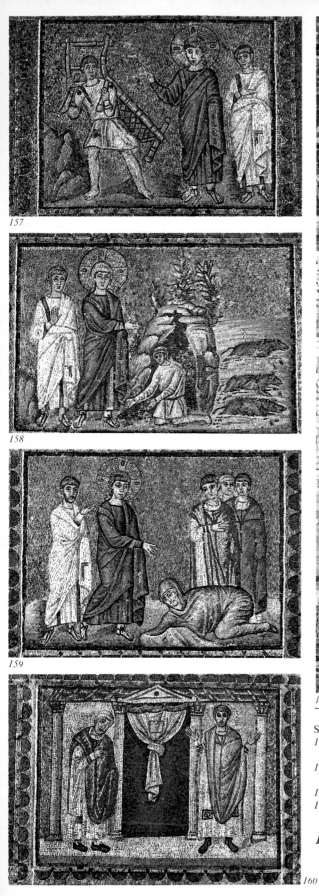

157

158

159

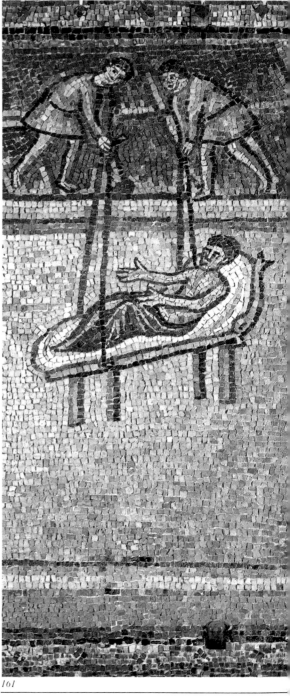

161

Small picture with scenes of miracles and parables of Christ:

157 - *The paralized Man of Bethesda now cured, carrying his bed.*

158 - *The healing of the madman (the evil spirits represented by the pigs).*

159 - *Christ indicates the scribes to the adulteress.*

160 - *The Pharisee prays with his lifted arms and the Publican beats his breast in front of the Temple.*

110

160

161 - *The paralized man of Capernaum is let down through the open roof in the house (detail).*

Small pictures with scenes of miracles and parables of Christ:

162 - *The Samaritan Woman at the Well (detail).*
163 - *The poor widow's mite.*
164 - *The Healing of the Blind Men at Jericho.*
165 - *The multiplication of the loaves and the fishes.*
166 - *The marriage at Cana.*

111

The right wall of the central nave

From the apse towards the front door, always in the upper part and alternated by motifs of the cross, two doors and a shell as in the wall opposite there are 13 small pictures about Christ's passion and Resurrection:

1) The Last Supper; 2) The Prayer in the garden at Gethsemane; 3) The kiss of Judas; 4) Jesus accompanied by the Disceples is lead to judgement; 5) Jesus before Caiaphas; 6) Jesus tells Peter he will deny Him three times); 7) Peter's Denial; 8) the Repentance of Judas: the restitution of money to Caifa; 9) Pilate washes his hands; 10) Jesus on the way to Calvary (Simon the Cyrenian carries the cross for Him); 11) the 2 Maries at the tomb with the Angel; 12) The Disciples' Walk to Emmaus; 13) Jesus reappears to the Apostles: the disbelief of Thomas (damaged by the bomb of 1916 also this picture was skilfully reconstructed by the Masters of the Mosaicists' Group of Ravenna).

All the small pictures are an exemplar demonstration of the high artistic quality reached by the mastery of Ravenna (in particular the scene of the Passion and Resurrection excel, both in the chromatic-series of the mosaic-material, and in the wealth of figures of Apostles, women, priests and scribes; Jesus is no longer the young man of the wall opposite, that is beardless and serene but His face is sad and with a full beard.

167

168

169

170

Small pictures of Christ's Passion and resurrection:

167 - *The Last Supper.*
168 - *The Prayer in the garden of Gethsemane.*
169 - *The kiss of Judas.*
170 - *Jesus accompanied by the Disciples is led to Judgement.*

113

173

Small pictures with scenes of Christ's
Passion and Resurrection:
171 - *Jesus before Caiaphas.*
172 - *Jesus tells Peter he will deny
Him (detail).*
173 - *Peter's Denial.*
174 - *The Repentance of Judas: the
restitution of money.*

115

174

175

176

177

178

180

In the part below, among the windows in the both walls of the nave, there are 16 images, always of Theodoric's time. These are statesque figures of high and solemn Saints and Prophets with a volume in their hands in different ways; covered with a white tunic and a white pallium. In the splayed-jamb of the right walls around the windows, there arc interesting geometrical motifs.

In the last and widest part, that is the lowest, beginning from the entrance the left, we can see the port and the town of Classe, with its embattled walls.

Two towers are in the entrance of the port and three big ships: one of these

---

Small pictures of Christ's Passion and Resurrection:
175 - *Pilate washes his hands (detail).*
176 - *Jesus on the way to Calvary.*
177 - *The Two Maries at the tomb with the angel.*
178 - *The Disciples' Walk to Emmaus.*
179 - *Jesus reappears to the Apostles.*
180 - *Image of the saint.*

117

181

has its sails unfurled. This representation is of Theodoric's time, the two figures which were before the first part of the walls and other three in the following part, have been chiselled away probably at the moment of the consacration of the Basilica to the catholic cult.

Later they were recovered, but with marble instead of the original glass paste taken from the mosaic of the castle's walls. One can see the shadow of such figures.

It follows the famous Procession of the 22 Virgins of Byzantine epoch: Eugenia, Sabina, Cristine, Anatolia, Victoria, Pauline, Emerenzia, Daria, Anastasia, Justine, Felicity, Perpetua, Vincenza, Valerie, Crispine, Lucy, Cecilia, Eulalia, Agnes, Agatha, Peladia and Euphemia.

Richly dressed and adorned with pearls and precious stones, they move towards the Madonna on the throne and the Child Jesus, having in their veiled hands the crown of the glory; the lawn is full of flowers, while palm's trunks are among their halos.

They are preceded by the three Wise Men who offer gifts to the Madonna.

During the last part, of Theodoric's time, unfortunately the upper part of the Wise Men was repainted by Kibel, who eliminated the crowns on their heads, replacing them with the Phrygian cap. This replacing followed the style of a similar image sculptured on the front of the sarcophagus 75th century) by the Bishop Isacio at the entrance of the Basilica of S. Vitale and on the Host-receptacle of S. Quirico and Giuditta in the Archbishop's museum.

Returning from the apse towards the main door, on the left, we see Christ the Redeemer, who appears majestic, seated on the throne with four angels (the third and the fourth angels have been badly restored by the Roman Kibel in 1852 who added arbitrarily the sceptre of Christ, too).

181 - The port of Classe (detail).
182 - The town of Classe with the embattled walls.
183 - Detail of the famous procession of the virgins.
184 - On pages 120-121: general view of the right side.

118

182

183

119

185

SCS MARTINVS✠SCS CLEM✠SCS

186

The 26 martyrs go towards the Redeemer.

They are: Martin (who the Basilica was dedicated to), Clement, Sixtus, Lawrence (who was the only one with the golden tubnic), Hippolitus, Cornelius, Cyprian, Cassiano, John, Paul, Vitale, Gervase, Protasio, Ursicino, Naborre, Felix, Apollinare, Sebastian, Demetrio, Policarpio, Vincent, Pancras, Crisogono, Proto, Hyacinth and Sabino.

The rhythmic march of the martyrs hasn't got the decorative abundance of the Virgins, because the only ornament is the whiteness of their garments. But in the hieretical gesture of the crown offered with veiled hands, re-asserts the harmony of the other procession, again rhythmic in the great leaves of the

---

185 - The Three Kings who offer gifts to the Madonna.
186 - Detail of the martyrs' procession (St. Martin with the golden tunic).
187 - Madonna with Child.
188 - The Redeemer Christ seating on the throne.

122

palms, rich in fruits, gifts of the martyrs. Near the main door, there is Theodoric's Palace.

The original Latin-icscription (Palatium) on the front part of the mosaic conferms that it is probably the Palace, built on the orders of Theodoric a few metres near the Basilica. We have no traces of it, except some very rich mosaic-floorings with marble inlayings. At the feet of the arches there is the «Victory».

Here it is very interesting to note the transformation from Arian in catholic church has given rise to the «purifications» as they were called - clearly visible to the naked eye. On the white of the Ist, 3rd, 5th and IIth columns of the palace one can see the hands or fingers and a forearm of not pleasant or even heretical personages.

The figures which represented

188

Theodoric on horseback was eliminated because they believed that an equestrian statue could adorned the palace itself.

We can also think that the Emperor of the East considered Theodoric as not more than a governor and not an independent King; the coins of that time had on the front the Emperor's image and on the back Theodoric.

Regarding from a religious point of view, even if there was not a great difference between Arian liturgical solemnities and catholic orthodox ones, the Arius heresy, which, spread in the IV century, didn't believe in the divinity of Christ and therefore in the Trinity: there was only one and unbegotten God for

187

PALATIVM

Arius. After the exam of the mosaic decoration, we must note the extremely simple apse, totally rebuilt during the post-war period (1950) on the original foundation of the VI century, instead of the baroque one, erected by the Franciscan Minor in 1612, which was enormous and in contrast with the semplicity of the original structure.

The 4 columns of porphyry are marvellous: the two in front have two Byzantine capitals in the shape of a basket, and the two behind have an Egyptian or rather an Alexandrian-school influence which are part in the ancient ciborium. Behind the VI century altar, there is the Roman marble table adorned on its sides with phitomorphic decorations.

The VI century pluteus is on the extreme left.

On the front it shows a decoration with peacocks and a rich vine decorated in leaves comes out of the cantharus on the back of the prophet Daniel in loin-cloth, above a vigorous plant of acanthus with two lions lied down alongside, referring to the Eucharist.

Also the three transennas (VI and VII century) are very interesting; they were finely fretworked because they were notably influenced by the Eastern out.

Even the marble ambo of the right aisle, presumably of the VI century, shows a mixture of classical and Oriental taste: as a matter of fact the ovolos and friezes* of the lower part are classical, and the geometrical motifs are of Constantinople.

On both sides there is the globe surmounted by a latin cross. The golden lacunar was built by the order of the Cardinal Caetani in 1611 to make it go better with the baroque apse which as we said before, was eliminated in 1950.

---

189 - The Theodoric's Palace.
190 - The socalled Theodoric's Palace.

The so-called
THEODORIC'S PALACE
(VIII century)

Although it was ascertained that this is the narthex of the church of St. Saviour of Calchi, tradition has continued to call this building Thodoric's Palace.

The building dates back approximately to the beginning of the VIII century with later additions (XIII century).

Nevertheless, the building took on its present form in the years between 1898 and 1900, while the tower which gives access to the upper floor, many pieces of floor-mosaics are exposed; some of these mosaics have a great importance because the imperial zone which was in the area between the present Via Alberoni and S. Apollinare Nuovo.

Theodoric's real Palace was therefore in this area. As told in the historical outline, it was devastated during the various raids of the Longobards, but it was completely stripped by Charles the Great with the consense of Pope Adrian I.

190

THE BASILICA OF S. MARIA IN PORTO
(XVIII century)

191

A great deal of the materials for the construction of this building were taken from the Basilica of St. Lawrence in Caesarea, which was thus finally demolished.

Begun in 1553, it was finished only in 1784 by the architect of Ravenna, Camillo Morigia who looked after in particular the upper part, adorning it with statues and columns.

In the façade, in the part below, there are 4 symbolic statues which are works of Cignaroli of Verona and represent: Charity, Fait, Hope and Humility.

In the centre on the main door we can see a Greek Madonna. The four statues of the upper part are by the same author: St. Augustine, St. Lawrence, St. Peter the Honests and St. Ubaldo. The interior, with a nave and two aisles, is Renaissance with columns alternated with pillars.

The left altar of the transept* has in the centre a small marble bas-relief which represents the praying Madonna called the **Greek Madonna** which is the object of a great cult by the people of Ravenna. The legend says that She

192

arrived on the beach on the 8th April 1100 at dawn, in the company of Angels. An oriental work it is XI century Byzantine even if its harmonious features and perfection remind one of Greek classical statues.

The large wooden **choir*** dating back to the end of the 16th century is really valuable.

193

One can see fragments of frescos of the Giottesque-Romagnese school. They are the remains of the great decoration, which was polverized during the 2nd world war bombardment of the town.

The Sarcophagus of Peter the Honest, the founder of the church, who liked to be called Peter the Sinner is absolutely fascinating. From the suburb of Porto Fuori one can arrive at the seaside (Lido Adriano, Punta Marina, Marina di Ravenna) going through the buill-up area and going on for 4 km along Via Staggi and Via Bonifica.

This Basilica stands out from the **Church of St. Maria in Porto Fuori** which is 6km from the town.

It was erected in the V century, but it was completely destroyed in the last war and later entirely rebuilt.

194

195

---

193 - *The Greek Madonna, object of great cult of the people of Ravenna.*

194 - *Porto Fuori: Church of S. Maria in Porto Fuori.*

195 - *Porto Fuori: Sarcophagus of Peter of the Honests, who is the founder of the Church.*

127

THE CLOISTER OF THE ANCIENT MONASTERY OF S. MARIA IN PORTO AND THE LOMBARDIC SMALL LOGGIA (XVI century)

At the beginning of the 16th century the Lateran Monks left the Monastery of S. Maria in Porto (6km from the town) and ordered the building in Ravenna of a new Monastery beside the Church which was again called S. Maria in Porto.

The works began in 1496 (the official date is 1502) when Leonardo Loredan was the doge.

The Monastery of Renaissance style of Venetian taste was the work of marble-workers of Lombardy and Campione. With the dissolution of the religious orders, it was transformed into quarters at first for the French troops and later for Austrians ones.

From 1815 it became a ware-house for which were gathered in the pine-woods of Ravenna. In 1885 it was nearby new large barrocks connected to, destroyed in the last war.

The Monastery, after its first restoration at the beginning of the century was completely rebuilt and restored by the town-hall. Its works, carried out by Ernesto Girelli of Ravenna, were finished in 1970.

From that period it has been the home of the town picture gallery and the school of fine arts which the Brandolini ornithological collection was added to.

The most interesting part of the building is the Loggia overlooking the Public Parks, in fact called «Lombardic small Loggia».

The architectural elements, which form the façade, are made of Istrian stones with some veined Greek marble columns. The large railings of the beginning if this century are beatiful.

In the interior there is the wide cloister with its pair of balconies.

For the visit of the picture gallery one must go upstairs to the 2nd floor.

---

196 - The Lombardic small Loggia seen from the Public Parks.

196

THE TOWN PICTURE GALLERY

It consists of the works of the gallery of the School of fine arts founded in 1829, that is 2 years after the opening of the school, in order to stimulate the young students. The vice pontifical legate Monsignor Lavinio Dè Medici Spada with the approval of the Gonfalonier Carlo Arrigoni succeded in persuading the rich and noble of Ravenna to leave on deposit several paintings.

Various charities and the closing-down of some state corporations provided the money for the acquisition of many great panel-works of ancient Romagnese teachers.

Unfortunately many paintings were withdrawn to be sold abroad. Nevertheless several works of great importance remained, including the very famous sepolcral statue of Guidarello Guidarelli.

In the tour we will note the most interesting paintings:

Ist small cella

SCHOOL OF BOLOGNA OF THE XIV CENTURY - S. Francesco who receives the stigmata among the St. Domenico, St. Rufino and S. Chiara.

This is a panel showing great realism with a good colonistic effect.

ANTONIO ALBERTI OF FERRARA (1423

St. Anthony Abbot

This is a part of a missing polyptych of refined esecution which was influenced by the School of Umbria and Marches of that period and vaguely of the school of Tuscany, in particular of Siena.

SCHOOL OF ROMAGNA OF THE XIV CENTURY

The Madonna on the throne with her Child in the centre; on the left, high up, there is the nativity below the Adoration; on the right high up there is the Crucifixion, below the Resurrection.

This is the most ancient painting of the collection (about 1340-1360); more powerful in the four lateral scenes, this unknown painter of Romagna reminds us widely of the school of Giotto and the school of Rimini.

ANTONIO ALBERTI OF FERRARA (1423)

St. Agostino

See the other panel of the same author.

SCHOOL OF MARCHES OF THE XV CENTURY

Madonna with Her Child

The author of the panel which summaries the experiences of a declining epoch, shows a lively sensitivity in its rhythmical subdivision.

GIOVANNI ANTONIO OF PESARO (XV CENTURY)

S. Peter Damiani

Attributed to Antonio of Fabriano, this panel is certainly interesting for its delicate colour-tones in particular the figures on the stole.

GROUP OF THE TEACHER OF STAFFOLO (XV CENTURY)

Crucifixion together with the Saints John Baptist Francis and Jerome

It is difficult to determine the author of this devotional small panel because of the mixture of the influences and stylistical basis. It is valuable for its delicate colouring.

ARCANGELO OF COLA OF CAMERINO (1416)

Christ Crucified betwen the Virgin and S. John

A spire of a polyptych, this small panel shows all the fertility of the school of the Marches which is filled with the culture of Tuscany.

2nd small cella

ANTONIO MARIA OF CARPI - BEGINNING OF THE XVI CENTURY

Madonna with Her Child;

This small panel, not without the influence of Palmezzano, is also attributed to the school of Cima of Conegliano.

MARCO PALMEZZANO (XVI CENTURY)

The nativity and the presentation at the temple and St. Martyr.

There are the remains of a painting; the first two parts are works with rare power; the composure and the composite rigour go well together with the noble serenity which comes out from the two scenes. The figure of the Saint is beatiful; this is a fragment of a more complex work.

3rd small cella

BIAGIO DANTONIO OF FLORENCE (END OF THE XV CENTURY)

Madonna with Her Child and S. Giovannino

This is attributed also to G. Battista Utili.

MATTEO DI GIOVANNI (1430-1495)

Madonna with Her Child between the St. Girolamo and Barbara.

This is an elegant work and subtle lyricism.

LORENZO MONACO (1370-1425)

Crucifixion

With the Crucifixion of Vivarini (5th small

cella) this is certainly the most important work of the Picture Gallery. Don Lorenzo di Giovanni of the convent of St. Maria degli Angeli of Florence known as Lorenzo Monaco painted this small panel about 1415. Its composition with elegant modulations and warm tones, constitutes an example of painting between International Gothic and Renaissance.

NICOLO DI LIBERATORE OF FOLIGNO KNOWN AS «THE STUDENT» (1425-1502)

Christ with the Cross and two Angels.

It is a painting of notable quality, permeated with resigned mysticism attributed to the last period of activity of th e painter of Umbria.

TADDEO OF BARTOLO (1362-1422)

The Archangel Gabriel and the Virgin

The sinuous rhythm of the drapery and the

197 - *Giovanni Antonio from Pesaro (S. Pier Damiani - XV century).*

198 - *Palmezzano Marco (Saint Martyr - XVI century).*

199 - *Alberti Antonio from Ferrara (S. Agostino - XV century).*

200 - *Antonio Vivarini: Crucefixion (XV century).*

enchantment which emanates from the expression of the Virgin set in gold, make these two works full of great interest.

SCHOOL OF PAOLO DI GIOVANNI FEI (LATE 1300 - EARLY 1400)
Crucifixion

The golden field on which the composition is set reminds us of the precious minatures of that period which add unreality with reality.

4th small cella

GENTILE BELLINI (1429-1507)
St. Peter and St. Lawrence

Only recently has this been attributed to such an author, son of the famous Jacopo and

brother of Giovannini.

5th small cella

ANTONIO VIVARINI (1415-1484)
Crucefixion

The delicate work of the founder of the school of Murano, shows a wise use of the space of the small table on which light and colour form a magical lyricism.

7th small cella

Some portraits of LUCA LONGHI (1507-1580) and his children BARBARA (1552-1638) and FRANCESCO (1557-1618) of Ravenna.

In the central corridor and in the room of

132

202

203

Guidarello Guidarelli there are other paintings of LONGHI, FRANCESCO ZAGANELLI (1465-1531) and NICCOLO RONDINELLI (1460-1515) painters who have been so far rather ignored by the critics.

Again in the central corridor there is the deposition, which is the great work of GIORGIO VASARI, the famous historian of Arezzo (1511-bià ù) which came from the Monastery of Classe.

Sepolcral Statue of Guidarello Guidarelli

When on 12th July 1823 the discendents and owners of the statue of Guidarello Guidarelli (Marianna Del Sale Spreti Giulio Rasponi and Antonia Del Sale Rasponi) approved that the sepolcral statue of Guidarello Guidarelli could be carried to the small oratory near S. Francesco, in the sculpture room of the School of fine arts, they would certainly not have imagined that it would become object of would wide interest, sometimes almost pathological.

Guidarello Guidarelli has been featured in many films and is the hero of a number of novels. Only recent research has shed some light on the real identify this man. A noble knight from Ravenna, born in Florence, in the service of Cesar Borgia, he was treacherously killed in Imola in 1501 by Virgil of Rome, who had borrowed from Guidarello Guidarelli a Spanish «camisa» and didn't want to give ti back to him.

Using the same words of the historian of that time: «Messer Guidarello da Ravenna, soldato dignitissimo del duca, abiando imprestato una sua camisa a la spagnola bellissima de lavori d'oro a Virgilio Romano a Imola per farsi mascara e non ie la volendo rendere e cruzatosi con lui, el ditto Virgilio lo taiò a pezzi e amazollo; el duca, fattolo piare, li fè taiar la testa».

The work was sculptured about 1525 by Tullio Lombardo, son of Peter, a shopkeeper, who worked in Venice and Ravenna at the end of 1400.

---

201 - *School of Cima from Conegliano (Madonna with Child - XV century).*
202 - *Matteo di Giovanni: Madonna with Childbetween the saints Jerome and Barbara.*
203 - *Lorenzo Monaco: Crucifixion (XIV century).*

133

204

All the interest of the work is concentrated in the face which contains reflections coming from the floor.

The eyes and the mouths, whith an impalpable sensuousness, seem imperceptibly to open at every movement of the beholder.

Lombardo's refined technique has permitted the transformation of the funeral mask into a bright surface with an extraordinary intensity.

In the room in the north there are: Paris Bordone (1500-1571): Christ the Redeemer; Sebastiano Mazzoni (1615-1685): the magnificent «Apollo and Daphne», a school of Fontainebleau (Teacher of Flora): allegory of the abundance; Rosa da Tivoli (1665-1701): The Herdsman.

In the corridor, provisionally there are the works of 1800, of the beginning of 19 and some contemporaries.

ORNITHOLOGICAL MUSEUM

The town collection which was named after its donor Brandolini of Ravenna, is rich in about 1600 examples of birdlife. About one thousand of them are the typical of the area to the south of Ravenna, between the Reno and Savio rivers from the beginning of the Apennines, going down towards the sea, with many plains, valleys and pinewoods.

Interesting birds are displayed, some of them are very rare or extint exotic birds, mammals and other naturalistic subjects. We hope they neither represent a *bygone* age, nor the acceptance of a lifeless nature, but an incentive to the visitor to become a defender of the nature that remains as a heritage for future generations.

The Museum, which is increasing its *stockand* becoming the Museum of Natural science for the town, ornithological library, and of an interesting shell - collection of Adriatic sea.

---

204 - *Tullio Lombardo - Sepolchral statue of Guidarello Guidarelli (XVI century).*

THOEDORIC'S MAUSOLEUM (VI century)

205

This is about one and a half kms from the centre of the town, north-eastwards, goingpast Brancaleone's castle, (a large military building of the Venetian time of the XV century, now a public garden and summer open-air theatre).

After the castle we turn right and cross the railway bridge. A large car-park makes the visit easy.

This building, mysterious because it was never completely understood, was erected by order of the gothic king Theodoric (died in 526) near the barbaric necropolis as his tomb.

Many legends talk about his death: he was kidnapped by a horse, thrown off a volcano went mad on seeing a victim of his inside the head of a fish was going to eat.

Teutonic tradition considered him a hero.

After many centuryes we see the far sightedness of his undertaking, raising Rome and its past in a moment in which its greatness was divided and exiled in distant Constantinople. This example of art of the late antiquity represents the power and the spirit of the gothic king very well.

The nearness of the Memorial Park, with its thicket of holms oaks, and cypress-trees, gives more power to the white and massive building of Istrian stone.

It was built using great squared blocks.

The spherical vault, still of Istrian stone is composed of only one block a metre thick, which is 33 metres in circumference and weigh about 280/300 tons.

The buiding appears to lean a little eastwards, even though it was built on a massive foundation.

If we consider that the monolith* was cut from the Istrian rocks and carried all this way across the Adriatic with an enormous raft, we can only wonder at enormousness of the undertaking.

---

205 - Theodoric's Mausoleum.

Originally the building was isolated, but after the Gothic domination a lighthouse was erected beside it (in that time the sea was very near and the port of Classe had been definetly abanduned).

A little before 1000, a monastery dedicated to S. Maria, took the Mausoleum, using it as an oratory.

So the Benedectine Convent was called S. Maria ad farum.

The Lighthouse with a square base has been lost ever since the XII century, and the Monastery was destroyed in the XVIII century. In the Middle Ages, this powerful building because a burial-place like the Pantheon of Rome.

Another necropolis (besides the original gothic one) was erected around it, and it was discovered in recent centuries. Until the middle of the XVIII century, the building was so ignored that the lower part was almost totally interred by the floods of the nearby river Badareno.

The work of reconstruction dates back to 1844, when the floor of the building was almost reached and in that

206

occasion many tombs were uncovered.

The mausoleum consists of two floors: the lower floor is decagonal with round niches, one of those is the access to the interior; the upper one, also decagonal is reached using a staircase and has an upper part with decorative pincer-motifs, typical of barbaric northern art.

The same decoration led to marvellous connections when a golden cuirass was found during the excavations in the dock in 1854. This cuirass was enriched with sparkling garnets, and it was called Theodoric's.

Unfortunately this cuirass, but perhaps only a rich harness for horses, was stolen from the National Museum in 1924 and never found again.

The twelwe «handles» which are sculptured upon the edge of the canopy apart from creating a plastic effect, were to make the canopies slide after assembly, probably using a pile of earth.

On the front of the so-called handles there are the names of the four Evangelists and the 8 Apostles carved, almost a symbolic ring of protection.

The interior of the ground floor in a shape of greek cross, is empty apart from a moulding* and 2 big unfinished shells in the eastern part and 2 also unfinished in the western part.

The upper floor, used by the Benedectines as an oratory, has a policrome cross in stucco on the monolithic block

207

---

206 - Decorative motif in a shape of a «pincer».
207 - Traces of the polychrome cross in stucco.
208 - Sarcophagus in a shape of a bath in porfyry.
209 - Detail of the external hollows and reliefs.

of the dome, which is considered to be the original one.

The starry sky, which probably covered the remaining surface, has disappeared. One can see the long split of the monolith, perhaps it forced the installation to be interrupted as one can see from the unsuccessful alignment of some features, for example the handles (previously mentioned) which are not symmetrically related to the western part.

One could think that it was upstairs because there is no staircase (and being upstairs it was protected from floods). Others retain that the funereal cell was downstairs, but the chapel upstairs.

The great sarcophagus in the shape of a bath (similar to the Roman ones of the IV century) of porphiry, in the so-called Theodoric's Palace and then National Museum, may have contained the mortal remains of the gothic king, but not for a long time, because the hate that Arianism and its leader caused in the othodox christians was fierce.

208

Before leaving this exceptional and unique monument dedicated to the fascinating and rather mystical figure of Theodoric, it is interesting to dwell upon another hypothesis relating to the monument.

This is the function of the external

209

hollows which are around the upper floor. The structures connected to these reliefs disappeared.

The most reliable hypothesis, which dates back to Sangallo, is that the hollows were part of an upstairs gallery supported by columns, which has now disappeared together with its columns. They were on the external side of the terrace which we go through, forming a circular colomnade.

THE BASILICA OF
S. APOLLINARE IN CLASSE (VI century)

To complete the visit of the mosaic-cycle of Ravenna, one must also see the Basilica of S. Apollinare in Classe, 5 km on the road from Ravenna to Rimini.

After the New Bridge over the United Rivers, on the edge of the town one can see from afar the bell-tower of the Basilica of Classe. On the left there is a flat plain, an expanse of cultivated fields the railway lines from Ravenna to Rimini regularly cross.

This area destined to become the future archeological park of Classe, contains much which is still be un-covered.

This area and especially the territory between Ravenna and Classe is really interesticg for archeological research.

Between Ravenna and Classe indeed there was the town of Caesarea with the beatiful Church of St. Lawrence in Caesarea (early V century) and dis-troyed in 1553 on the orders of Julius II to salvage the building-material.

Regarding the archeological park, we hope that the remains of the port, streets, factories, stores, public and private buildings and expecially the large necropolis (are finally found out with a great variety of tombs, from the simple stele to the mausoleum in the shape of a round tower) which includes all the cemeterial areas with their relative churches, which were erected during 10 centuries of settlement.

The limited available surface of the dunes, sea-floods and the laying underground have formed a stratification which has created a division of this long period of history, not only of Ravenna.

Her is a detail about the churches of the various cemetery-areas: in the middle of the road between Ravenna and Classe one can see the remains of St.

Severus (VI century) with the ruins of the bell-tower with a square base; the Basilica Probi (in the middle of the VI century) 200 metres from the Basilica of S. Apollinare, the vanished Church of S. Eleucadio and the Basilica Petriana (early V century) erected by S. Pier Crisologo (Peter I Crisologo).

This concentration of great churches doesn't surprise us: Christianty arrived first in the territory of Classe, in the interior of the cosmopolitan community composed of eastern elements (Syrian, Judaean, Egyptian and expecially Greek elements).

Not by chance the first Bishop of Classe was St. Apollinaris from Antioch and not by chance the first bishops resided in Classe and only later did they move to Ravenna.

The Basilica of S. Apollinare in Classe, the largest early Christian Basilica was erected on the orders of Bishop Ursicino using the money of the banker Julian the silversmith (the mysterious and very rich Greek who almost at the same time ordered the construction of the Basilica of S. Vitale). This was finished and consacrated later on May 8th, 549 as can be seen from an ep graph, which has now disappeared by the Bishop Maximian and dedicated to the first Bishop of Classe.

The Basilica was certainly erected next to a Christian cemetery. In 1756 the Camaldolesians found a great deal of pagan funeral steles which had been re-used in Christian buildings showing that a short time before there was a previous pagan necropolis.

The **large façade** presents two simple uprights and one mullioned window with three openings.

The narthex was reconstruction as well as the buildicg in the shape of the tower on the left.

The **round bell-tower** (37.50 m high) dating back to the X century was fortunately rescued in the last world war, both from the anglo-american air-bombardments and from the destruction ordered by the Allied Command. (because it had become an observation point for the German Army), and from the German mines in retreat. The consequences for the Basilica are easily imaginable.

This is the most beautiful bell-tower in Ravenna, because of the alternation of red and yellow brick diamond design always and the progression of narrow loopholes which are in two orders of mullioned windows with one opening, one of windows with two openings and three of windows with three openings.

The interior

In the interior we have a marvellous sight: the rhythm created by the 24 columns of magnificent Greek transver-

211

---

210 - *Basilica of S. Apollinare in Classe.*
211 - *Emperor Caesar Augustus, the founder of the port of Classe (in the back the bell-tower of the Basilica).*

sally veined-marble ends in the delicate green of the mosaic-meadow, in the whiteness of the sheep, in the shining of the pine-wood of S. Apollinare.

All this in perfect unity between architecture and decoration of exceptional importance for the history of Christian* art. The columns are supported by a showy socle almost in the shape of a cube and a capitals are in the shape of a turgid acanthua leaves, but lightened by a fine fretwork.

The faded frescos of the wall of the central nave, representing some of the archbishop of Ravenna, date back to the XVIII century.

The lateral walls, which are now bare, were not certainly so, when the Basilica was opened.

Unfortunately in 1449 Pandolfo Sigismondo Malatesta, allied to the Venetians ordered the transport of «Hundreds of cartloads» of valuable marbles from S. Apollinare in Classe to Rimini, when Leon Battista Alberti used them to adorn the façade of the Malatesta-Temple.

It is likely the episode has been exaggerated by the chronicle which was written later, but the damage to the Basilica was very real.

The apse

The mosaics of the apse are witnesses to the last cycle of the mosaic-art of Ravenna even though some parts belong to the later periods.

High at the centre of the triumphal arch, there is the bust of the Christ with a halo and with the right hand blessing.

On the both sides in a multitude of coloured clouds there are the wings-symbols of the four Evangelists with the bull with the nostrils in the front (IX century).

Twelve sheep (the Apostles) advance upwards symmetrically, six on each side, towards Christ in the mountain; they come out from Jerusalem and

212 - Interior: view of the central nave.

Bethlem: the arch of the history of the man's salvation.

The attribution of the period of esecution of this mosaic-part is, however, uncertain.

Below on each side there are two high palm-trees are the symbol of martyrdom.

Lower, on the right, the Archangel Gabriel and, on the left, the Archangel Michael carry the banner bearing the praises of the Thrice Holy God in Greek.

Again lower we see the figures on both sides, one with the indication «St. Mattew» of late execution, and perhaps between the XI and XII centuries.

The undersides of the arch is decorated with birds and plants in a great golden wealth.

In the apsidal conch, we can see the hand of God with clouds going out showing the cross, alluding to the transfiguration of Christ on Mt. Tabor.

The great jewelled and golden cross with the head of Christ in the middle., is in a sky sprinkled with 99 golden and silver-stars alluding to the parable of the 99 sheep.

At the ends of the arms of the cross the letters Alpha and Omega indicate the beginning and the end of the course of the man's life.

Beneath the cross we read the words: «Salus Mundi» i.e. Salvation of the World, and above the Greek words «Fish» meaning «Jesus Christ Son of God Saviour».

The presence of these Greek words clearly proves that the people of Classe were deeply imbued with Greek culture.

The prophets Elijah on the right, and Moses on the left among many cirruses have beside them three lambs which represent the Apostles Peter, James and John as witnesses of the Transfiguration. On a shining green meadow which expresses the joy of all nature for the salvation of Christ, rich in lilies, daisies, olive trees, cypressuses, pines, birds and rocks.

The figure of the praying Archbishop St. Apollinaris stands out, with the ancient bishop's pinewood and the Bishop's pallium. The way in which everything is out of all proportion must be noted with great interest. We note flowers a high as trees, enormous lambs in an abstraction which anticipated the art of the Middle Ages. One can see a red line which contains an excellent remaking of the mosaic-restorer Zampiga of Ravenna at the beginning of the century.

Among the windows one can find most ancient decoration, because it is undoubtly contemporary with the erection of the Basilica. We can see the figures representing the Bishops of Ravenna Ursicinus, Ursus, Severus and Ecclesius in their sacred vestments with books in their hands who are indicating the presence of the word of Christ.

Beside the base of the triumphal arch two widely damaged scenes are portrayed: on the right we see the three sacrifices of the Old Testament Abel, Abraham and Melchizedeck, that is the Eucharist.

On the left (referring to the two panels of S. Vitale with the imperial offering of Justinian and Theodora) there are the Emperor Constantine IV Pogonatus with his brothers Heraclius and Tiberius III and Justinian III, in the act of offering the rescript of Privileges for the Church of Ravenna to Reparatus, the delegate of Archbishop Maurus.

This image partly distempered imitating the mosaic, dates back to the XII century.

These two last scenes display the decline of the art of Ravenna which had become almost lifeless.

The **Crypt**, accessibile because it has been recently restored and perfectly protected from the water which constantly penetrated it, dates back to the IX century.

The vault composed of salvaged stone has a semicircular trend with a

142

214

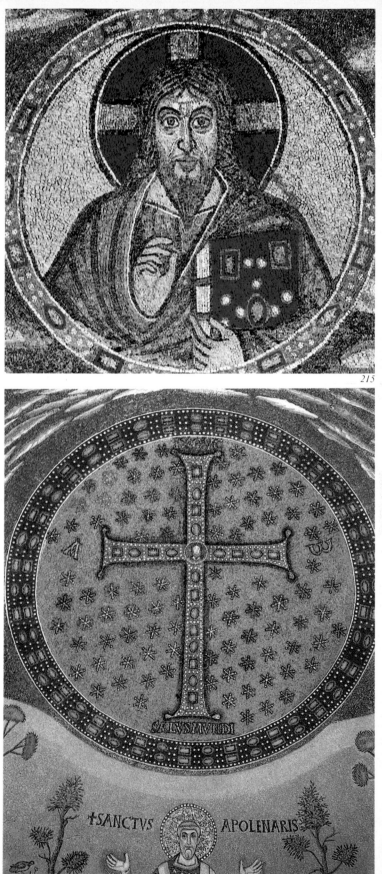

215

216

213 - *Suggestive view of the apse.*
214 - *Archangel Gabriel.*
215 - *The haloed Christ with the right blessing hand.*
216 - *Begemmed and golden cross with in the middle the face of Christ.*

143

perpendicular cell. In the cell there is a marble tomb which, it is written in the inscription, twice contained the remains of St. Archbishop Apollinaris.

At the bacf of the two lateral aisles beside the apse we see two ancient chapels, (prothesis and diaconicon) restored in 1906. In the left aisle there is one of the most famous examples of Christian canopy, which is from the vanished church of Ravenna St. Eleucadios.

217 - Detail of the face of Christ in the large begemmed cross.
218 - Detail of the palm, symbol of the martyrdom.
219 - Archangel Michael.
220 - S. Mattew (detail).
221 - The prophet Elijah.
222 - The prophet Moses.

217

218

219

221

222

220

✝SANCTVS APOLENARIS

223 - *The Archbishop S. Apollinaris.*

224 - *Detail of the apse.* ▶

225 - *The bishop of Ravenna Ursici-*
no.

226 - *The three sacrifices of the Old*
Testament: Eucharist.

227 - *The Emperor of the East Fla-*
vio Constantine IV Pagonato.

226

227

229

Its construction which dates back to the XI century, is not of course ideal, because it is difficult to see all of it.

This is a well preserved example of the Italic sculpture with motifs of helix, peacocks, doves and vines.

The canopy has spiral-shaped columns.

On the small frontal arch we learn that it was erected under Bishop Valerius (806).

The opposite floor with a multicoloured mosaic, derives from the original flooring and it has been recently restored by the group of the Mosaicists, who have also restored a part of the apse.

The small altar in the middle of the church was dedicated by Abbot Ursus to the Virgin and the remains of the Saint were found below it in 1173.

---

228 - Canopy of S. Eleucadio (IX century).
229 - Side of the sarcophagus of S. Theodore (V century).
230 - Sarcophagus of the bishop Theodore (V century).
231 - Sarcophagus with six niches (end of the V century).
232 - Sarcophagus of the lambs (end of the V century).

151

230

231

PINE-WOODS AND VALLEYS AROUND RAVENNA

The origin of the pine-woods can be dated back to the Roman period, when the communities around the port of Classe planted some pines within the limits of the **ancient coastal forest of Ravenna** which included the floristic and vegetational elements of the large Po-forests.

The largest extension (about 7,000 hectares) was reached by the pine-woods in 1700 after vast coastal reforestation, carried out patiently by the monastic orders which were the owners of the luxuriant forest. Towards the end of 1800, the towns of Cervia and Ravenna became the owners of the historical pine-woods, when many fellings of their areas had been concluded and soon after some hard winters destroyed a great deal of old pines.

The felling of the pine-woods of Savio, Porto and S. Giovanni had split the splendid arch of «thick, alive and divine forest» created on the Etruscan-Roman coast, and reduced to more than 2.000 hectares the pine-wood of Cervia, at the Southern extremity of Classe and S. Vitale, respectively to the south and north of the town of Ravenna. At the beginning of this century, the transformation of the natural renvironment of Ravenna, as well in the other parts of Italy had intervened only to conquer lands destined to agriculture.

The drainage had already induced the reclamation of vast valleys, but nevertheless many thousands of hectares of marshes remained. They were the remains of the vaster marshes which had given life the rivers Reno and Lamone, which for centuries had spread their waters along the coast of Romagna. Nowadays only the **Valli di Argenta** (Ferrara) and near Ravenna the 450 hectares of the splendid marsh of **Punte Alberete and Valle della Canna** survive.

Again at the beginning of this century there was on the east of the coast of

233 - Corner of pine-wood.

Ravenna a large lagoon, separated from the sea by a littoral sandy cordon, which the sea and the wind had formed in the course of the last centuries, using the detritus coming from the soil erosion, accelerated after the vast deforestation.

However, even if later and in a lesser extent, this lagoon had to suffer the agriculture drainage which has reduced and broken it up in the present *«pialasse (¹) del Piombone»* (now largely transformed by industrial installation) of the *«Risega»* and *«Baioni»* (the largest and the most important in a naturalistic sense, situated in the east of the pine-wood S. Vitale) and of the wet a e's of the *«Ortazzo and Ortazzino»*, in the East of the pine-wood of Classe.

In the first years of the century, the Senator Luigi Rava, an eager and far-sighted politician of Ravenna, together with the great lgve of the people for the pine-wood, passed some simple laws and created on the new littoral cordons a zone of dunes, owned by the state, which every year the sea would have enlarged with new *relics*.

On thes relics a new coastal pinewood would grow up with the possibility of going eastwards, which for the intervening geological happenings, had previously been prevented and then it would build a continuous green *«decoration»* along the coast of Ravenna.

Nevertheless, two things at that time couldn't and were not forseen: first of all the fashion of going for a swim would involve, in the following decades, a great deal of people and workers creating new towns on the seaside which were formed from the small settlements of the fishermen and the widening at the expense of the pine-woods.

Secondly, a natural happening amplified by the work of man (pumping

(¹) Pialassa derives from «pia» and «lassa»: take and leave, that is a zone which is periodically taken and left by the waters because of the tide.

water and gas from the subsoil) - subsidence - would induce the sea not to build, but to erode the coast raising the problem of defending the tourist residential settlements and the Pine-woods of State from the sea-floods.

This brief summary of the last happenings of the area of Ravenna appeared essentially to explain, even if only a little the present distribution, the state and the preciousness of the surviving natural environments, where the tourist must not seem a further element of degradation.

On the contrary, he must rather represent a reason for a better and more rigid conservation of an unrepeatable heritage, which is still threatened.

Now we will indicate some itineraries, which we consider more representative, in a way to offer emotions and beauty of images even to visitors who are not particularly prepared for the comprehension of natural facts, but any way open to rispect and observation.

PUNTE ALBERETE - VALLE DELLA CANNA

At about two km from Ravenna, we drive into the Main road Romea, which leads to Venice. After 9.5 km we see on the left a small car park.

We remind you that you can only enter the out parts of Punte Alberete using the carriage-road «Scagnarda» which divides it in two parts, in the southern area of the river Lamone, and only from sunrise till sunset.

On the contrary, a special permit is essential for access to the interior of the oasis.

(Ravenna town council - Heritage Department).

The district of **Punte Alberete - Valle della Canna** represents, as we have said. the last great sweet-water marsh, which is a part of the «cassa di colmata» of the river Lamone.

This river, which a long time ago was a swamp in a very large area and only a

234

235

The two areas have the same geological nature and in conclusion this nature is the same as the adjacent Pinewood of S. Vitale from which the district is now separated by the North Romea motorway.

This geological nature is a succession of ancient cordons of dunes with a sandy structures «shaft» more or less parallel to the coast-line and of interposed low positions partly full of river mud.

This structures is evident in **Punte Alberete** where the level of the water, which is drawn from the Lamone and used for the protectionistic aims, leaves uncovered or submerges only periodically the «shafts» where thick woods are growing.

On the contrary in **Valle della Canna** the «shafts» are not apparent where the water level is kept very high for aims of hydrodrinkable reserve.

A few metres from the car parks there is a path which borders a channel of artificial excavation and winds in the thicker part of the woods. In the space a few hundred metres the visitors can contemplate in opposite order, the success of the evolutional phase which, from the cane brake through the formations into

few years ago was again «canalized» to the sea, divides now the southern part of the marsh, the **Punte Alberete** from the **Valle della Canna** or **Valle Mandriole**, to the north of the river.

This swamp has been saved in the last moment by draining, thanks to the intervention of the newborn protectionist movement of Ravenna of that time.

Now thanks to the continuous fight of some naturalists of this movement, this swamp was enjoed from 1977 the prohibition of hunting and a system of management which has prevented the cutting of wood and allowed the free evolution of the valuable vegetational elements.

willow (Salix Caprea), white willow (Salix alba), ashtree and white poplar (Fraxinus excelsior and populus alba), and lead to the **Wood of Farnia** (Quercus robur) which represents the point of arrival of the evolutional trend for those environmental conditions.

During the tour even on small bridges, we go through splendid swampy areas which in nympholas and branches, coinciding with the old shafts of Slow (Prunus Spinosa) and wild pear (Pirus piraster) covered in marvellous white flovers in the spricg. **Punte Alberete** is a shelter for rare species of insects, Anphibiouses (such as the Lataste frog - Latastei frog) and rectiles already vanished from the wide areas where along time ago they lived such as the swamp tortoise (emys orbicularis).

More over it has one of the most important «wooded swamps» (Areas of nest-building of one or more species of herons) of Italy with hundreds of nest of little egrest (Egretta garzetta) night herons (Nycticorax Nycticoras) of the rare squacco heron (Ardeola ralloides) and for two years also of one or two couples of the pygmy cormorant (Phalacrocoras pygmaeus): this is the only place where it is present in western Europe.

Keeping to the path and not breaking the prohibition of access is essential to avoid troubling the colony of birds and allowing that the oasis continues its aims of protection.

The observation of the birds will be easier and without any trouble. They stop in great quantities and move in the large «lights» among the cane-brakes of **Valle della Canna**.

236

237

238

---

234 - *Partial view of the «Valle della Canna».*
235 - *The pine-wood of S. Vitale near Punte Alberete.*
236 - *Punte Alberete: the blooded forest.*
237 - *The nest-builder penduline titmouse on a branch of white willow.*
238 - *Flowers of nymphaea.*
239 - *A small flock of little Egrets.*

155

240 - The purple heron.

Whoever stops beside the main road, near the bridge on the Lamone at 2,300 m from the carpark of Punte Alberete, contemplates every season the marvellous spectacles of several species of ducks, herons, the flights of the marsh-harrier (circus aeruginosus) and the osprey (Pandion haliaetus), too.

A visitor interested in the natural aspects of the territory of Ravenna can't omit one or more visits to the pine-wood of Ravenna. Of course we refer to the **historical pinewoods of Classe and S. Vitale** which either from the scientific point of view or the scenic one, have the greatest interest and represent one of the rare example of plain-forest, which has survived in our country.

In order to avoid fire damage access to cars is permitted only after a special town-permission.

Then, from the middle od May to the middle of October even access to pedestrians is forbidden (except for special personal permission). **The parks** are, on the contrary, always accessible: «Ist of May» (pinewood of Classe, at Fosso Ghiaia, 5km from the town, on the Adriatic main road towards Rimini), «2nd of June» (Pinewood of S. Vitale, on the main road North Romea towards Venice, 8 km from the town), «25th of April» (near the river Lamone).

PINEWOOD OF S. VITALE

One of the itineraries which we recommand you, is a short crossing from west to east and back, of the pinnewood of S. Vitale, starting from the Carraia of the ca' Vecchia, which starts in front of the carpark of Punte Alberete. The wood begins from the road edges with great examples of oaks and ash-trees on lands which are partly marshy.

It is important to remember that before the building of the North Romea road there was a real continuity between the wood of Punte Alberete and the wood of S. Vitale.

Moreover this part of the wood overlooking the road had already concluded that transformation from pine-wood to broadleaves wood which more or less rapidly the entire forest of Ravenna would tend to do.

The underwood of the pine-wood is certainly the more authentic and interesting part, rich in dozens of species of shrubs and lianas as the whitehorn (Crataegus monogyna) the common privet (Ligustrum vulgare) the dogwood (Cornus sanguines), corneltree (Cornus mas) the alder Buckthorn (Rhamnus frangula), the Buckthorn (H Rhamnus catharticus) the water elder (Viburnum opulus) the fillirea (Philyrea augustifolia), the butcher's broom (Ruscus aculeatus) the asparagus (Asparagus acutifolius) the scorpion senna (Coronilla emerus), the spindle tree (Evonimus europaeus) and many others which fill the air with incredible perfumes with their flowers and at the end of the summer, shows off their vivacious fruits.

The pinewood appears black in the highest shafts of dunes, surrounded by the most perfumed bushes of the underbrush. Along the grassy path and in the clearings of the underwood, in the late spring there are dozens of species of small, but splendid orchids some of them really rare.

Pietro Zangheri, the famous materialist and botanist, of the Romagna, has described more than 900 species of plants for the wood of Ravenna and the neighbouring territories.

Going on beyond the «Ca' Vecchia» we see the splendid «**Bassa del Pirottolo**» which is a swampy area which crosses in a longitudinal sense a great part of the pinewood of S. Vitale.

It rapresents a hollow of dunes which was in ancient times connected to one of the river-ways, probably joined to the branch of the Po of Padusa (or Padenua, from which, maybe the name of Ravenna originated), which had in Etruscan-Roman times a great part in the formation of the coastal area of the Romagna.

When you have finished crossing the pine-wood, jou arrive on the edge of the Piolassa of the Baiona: beyond the wide lago on there is the littoral pine-wood of the State and the town Marina Romea.

241 - Orchid in bloom.

242 - Pine-wood of S. Vitale: the «Bassa of the Pirottolo».

157

GLOSSARY

Acanthus - Plant with wide leaves from the East which, according to the legend, suggested to the Athenian Callimachus, the motif of the Corinthian capital, very used in Greek and Roman decoration.

Acroterium - Decorative or figurative element which surmounts the summit and the edges of the pediment.

Aedicula - Small temple constructed to protect a statue.

Altar-frontal - Liturgical covering of the altar which hides the anterior part of the mensa.

Ambo - Pulpit; which is on the ground and with raised floor. It is used for reading the gospel which is leaned on the lectern.

Ambulatory - Secondary room, usually with a very long portico.

Apse - Back well of the church with a semicircular or poligonal plan. In its interior it corresponds to the choir, which is the end of the central nave.

Barrel vault - Space determined by the arch on small columns or piers.

Base - Lower end of the column. Generally it is composed of a parallelepipedon with a square plan, or a prism with a poligon plan, on which lean the shaft of the column rests.

Bas-relief - Sculpture on a flat surface from which the figures stand out only a little. No part is completely separate from the flat surface. (Unlike the kind of bas-relief, which even if there is a minimum projection, we have a sensation of great depth).

Bell-tower - Vertical tower of a church containing the belfry at the top. It seems to originate from lighthouses and Roman towers.

Byzantine - Style which is fluorished-during the Roman Empire of the East between the IV century and the XV century A.D. It is the eastern Christian art. It is named after Byzantine (which Constantine called Constantinople). Fundamental charachteristics are: regarding the architecture, there is a preference for the central plan rather than the basilican rectangular one, the great dome to which all the other elements are subordinate and the use of details resulting from the fusion of motifs of late classicism with the Persian and Syrian ones. Regarding sculpture and pictures there is a strong decorative sense: bas-reliefs and mosaics adorn the various architectural parts, magnificence and pure colour are prevailing elements.

Canopy - Baldachin generally supported by columns, which covers the altar with symbolic protection.

Cantharus - Big vessel with two handles used for drinking.

Capital - The top of the column.

Catechumens - Whoever, converted to Christianity, prepares himself to receive the Baptism.

Cathedral - Church in which there is the Bishop's throne.

Chasuble - Ancient name of the priest's planeta.

Chlamys - Regal mantle (symbol of authority).

Choir - Part of the church wich corresponds to the apse.

Christian (style) - Characteristical style of the period from the end of the Ist period A.D. to the end of the VI century. The Christian style contains western classical elements and eastern elements as well. In Ravenna which was the new capital of the Western Roman Empire, the fusion created the style of Byzantius and Ravenna.

Clipeus - It originates from the shield used by Roman Militia.

Colonnade - Succession, order of columns arranged in a building.

Column - Architectural elements formed by a vertical cylinder, which supports the arches or architrave; sometimes it is only an ornament.

Corbel - Supporting stone for the edges of the vaults.

Corinthian - Greek and Roman architectural order, of which the column has a capital adorned with a double or triple order of acanthus' leaves or alive or lotus' leaves.

Crypt - Underground room generally under the church, where there are tombs and relics.

Diaconicon - Small sacristy leaning against the apse of the Basilica of Ravenna (S. Apollinare in Classe) for the service of the officiants.

Episcopal throne or seat - It is generally situated in the middle of the apse of the Christian Basilicas.

Estrados - External (convex) surface of an arch or vault.

Festoon - Decorative, classic, ancient and Renaissance motif with a form of a garland of flowers or fruit.

Frieze - Space put between the architrave and the cornice. It is often adorned.

Greek fret - Decoration formed by a band, which with right angles changes continually and rythmically the direction.

High-relief - Sculpture made on a flat surface, but in great relief so that the figures stand out from the flat surface.

Intrados - Internal (concave) surface of an arch or a vault.

Lacunar - Hollowed compartment, which is poligonal very used in ceilings, vaults and domes.

Lunette - Space in a 1/2 circle or mixtilinear triangle shape situated between a base and the rest of the vaults.

Mensa - Altar table.

Monolith - Stone or construction represented by only one block of material.

Moulding - Decorative element which stands out from the shaft of the wall. It has a continual trend. Its standing out from the wall is named «projection».

Narthex - Portico in front of the ancient Christian Basilicas very used in the VI century, like the pronaos. The catechumens not admitted to the interior of the church gathered here.

Nave - Longitudinal space of a church, divided by rows of the columns or pilasters.

Niche - Hollow in the thickness of the wall, usually destined to hold a statue.

Nimbus - Halo

Pallium - Ancient mantle worn by the ancient Greeks and Romans; in liturgy dressed on the planeta.

Paten - Metal-plane with a large border used to cover in the chalice and to hold the Host.

Patera - Plain and round vase, which as used in ancient times for the libations made in funerals.

Pianeta - Liturgical outer tunic worn by the priest to celebrate Mass.

Pilaster - Support which a square or rectangular section.

Pilaster-strip - Part of pilaster leaning against the wall, with purely decorative function.

Pinnacle - Crowning point with a triangular form of a building or part of it.

Pluteus - Parapet decorated with historical scenes of wooden or metal and often stone which define the altar, the choir or the presbytery.

Portal - Large and rich church door.

Pronaos - Small hall near the entrance of the Romanesque and Gothic churches, of which the frontal arch is supported by the columns.

Prothesis - Small room beside the apse; sacristy of the presbyters.

Pulvin - Architectural element which stands about the Byzantine capital on which the arch leans.

Quadriportico - Quadrangular porticade in front of the Christian Basilicas; the side attached to the façade is called a narthex.

Sacellum - Small chapel.

Splayed-jamb - Thickness of a wall around a window of door (see Church of S. Agatha at the end of the 3rd paragraph).

Thurible - Censer or vessel in which incense is burnt in churches (see St. John Evangelist where mosaics as a popular subject are dealt with - Fox's funeral).

Transenna - Parapet decorated with fretwork, motifs, partywall, balustrade.

Transept - Trasversal nave of a church. It forms with the main nave the Latin cross or the Greek one.

Truss - Wooden or iron triangular structure with the aim of supporting the roof.

Tympanum - Triangular space among the curnice of the frontispiece.

Underarch - Interior part of an arch.

Vault - Curved covering in the interior of a church or rooms and so on.

INDEX

Presentation	p.	2
An outline of the hystory	p.	3
The mosaic	p.	8
Piazza del Popolo	p.	10
1st ITINERARY	p.	13
Galla Placidia Mausoleum	p.	14
The Basilica of S. Vitale	p.	26

The mosaics of the Presbytery p. 31 The apse mosaic p. 50.
Justinian p. 52. Theodora p. 56.

The National Museum	p.	61
The Church of S. Maria Maggiore	p.	69
The Church of Santa Croce	p.	69
2nd ITINERARY	p.	70
Tomb of Dante	p.	71
St. Francis	p.	73
The Church of St. Agatha	p.	77
The Archbishop's Museum and Chapel	p.	78
The Neonian or Orthodox Baptistry (or Baptistry of the Cathedral)	p.	86
The Cathedral	p.	92
3rd ITINERARY	p.	95
The Church of Spirito Santo	p.	96
The Arian Baptistry	p.	97
Basilica of S. Giovanni Evangelista	p.	101
Basilica of S. Apollinare Nuovo	p.	104

The left part of the central nave. p. 108
The right part of the central nave p. 112

The so-called Theodoric's Palace	p.	125
Basilica of S. Maria in Porto	p.	126
The cloister of the ancient Monastery of S. Maria in Porto and the small Lombardic Loggia	p.	128
The town picture gallery	p.	129
The sepolchrale statue of Guidarello Guidarelli	p.	133
The Ornithological Museum	p.	134
The Theodoric's Mausoleum	p.	135
Basilica of S. Apollinare in Classe	p.	138
Pine-woods and Valley around Ravenna	p.	152

Punte Alberete - Valle della Canna p. 153
Pine-wood of S. Vitale p. 156

Glossary	p.	158

Printed at the
Fotometalgrafica Emiliana printing press.
S. Lazzaro di Savena (Bologna)
february 1987